Blogging Secrets

An Uncommon Guide to Generating Six Figures on the Internet, Escaping the 9-5 and Living the Dot Com Lifestyle

John Chow and Peng Joon

Table of Contents

Preface

When we first set out to write this, the goal was to provide a comprehensive look into the techniques we both use to create compelling, money-making blogs that are both highly popular and content-rich, and that effectively generate streams of income.

In the time since we started writing, a lot of things have changed. We have learned more about what people are actually struggling with, which helped us realize how we can enhance and approach the topic of teaching people how to blog in an organic, down-to-earth way - one that ends with a nice income stream.

The advice in this book refers mostly to my blog JohnChow.com and the content and sites created by me over the course my career as one of the web's top bloggers. At the same time you will receive insights into online marketing, affiliate marketing and developing income streams online that come straight from Peng Joon's multi-million dollar portfolio of online businesses.

Together we have joined forces to create this book with the express purpose of showing you how it is possible to use exceptionally high-quality content and an eager audience to create a search-engine friendly website that can make you a tremendous amount of money - all from the comfort of your own home.

Enjoy, and here's to seeing you online in the very near future!

John Chow and Peng Joon

Introduction

You're about to embark on a journey I stumbled upon more than 13 years ago and that today has made me a very successful, well respected man in a massive niche.

To be perfectly honest with you, I still don't quite understand how it happened. How a simple kid from Canada created one of the largest and most successful blogs on the Internet and how today I make more than $30,000 a month from a blog, working from home on my own terms.

It's quite literally the "dream" that everyone talks about and I'm living it.

This book is about how to turn your dreams into real, tangible goals, because I know everyone reading this wants the same things - success and happiness in your life. But, for that dream to become a reality, you need to stop waiting for "some day" and start acting today to make them a reality.

That means setting tangible goals, acting on those goals and working towards something in the future. That's what I did and what I want to show you how to do in the coming days.

Who is John Chow?
If you haven't heard of me or don't know anything more than that I post content about blogging and making money online, here's a little bit of background.

In 1999 I started a website to document the computer I was building. I got lucky and landed some traffic early on from a forum I was a member of and eventually converted that simple webpage into what amounted to a very early-style blog - a review site for computer parts and components called The Tech Zone.

I worked tirelessly on The Tech Zone for more than 12 years and it went through numerous iterations - from Version 2 in 1999 when I started promoting Maximum PC Network products and earning thousands of dollars per month, to Version 3 a few months later and the $1.3 million offer I got for the site, just before the dotcom bubble popped.

The first few years I spent online were a whirlwind. I wrote reviews of video cards and motherboards and made a killing. But like all Internet success stories, everything soon came crashing down because of the severely mismanaged nature of Internet businesses, including the affiliate network I had been making so much money from and the advertisers who had been filling my coffers.

That's where I stayed for 2-3 years, waiting out the dotcom bust and making enough to pay my bills. It wasn't until 2003 when Google surged onto the scene with AdSense that I started making real money again.

June 18, 2003 - that's when AdSense launched and when I started posting huge volumes of click throughs that converted to hard cash in my pocket. By the end of 2004, the advertising business online was back where it had dropped off in 2000, and it never looked back.

I revamped my site again and continued growing my business. I also met the woman of my dreams, Sarah, and eventually got married - something that would not have been possible had I worked a normal 9-5 job.

The lesson behind all this is that the Internet is not a stable force. It changes. People make poor decisions and they fail, but it is those who stick with it, have clear goals and know what they want out of their businesses that will persevere through it all.

Who is Peng Joon?

In 2004, I was flat out broke. I had spent my college years addicted to computer games. In truth, I nearly flunked out but still managed to scrape by.

Post-graduation nobody wanted to hire me. To make matters worse I had been on a conditional scholarship from the government and because my results were so poor, I now had to pay back RM153,000 (approximately USD 50,000). I was unemployed, broke and in debt.

Securing a good job was near impossible with my college results, so after three months of searching I settled for a job selling credit cards. I managed to make a grand total of two sales. My mom. And my dad.

After hopping around odd jobs, I settled for a "stable" job, as a financial consultant. My monthly salary was a measly RM1,200 (approximately USD 400) and I stayed there for over a year and a half. I realized that it was going to take me over 30 years to fully pay off my study loan if I remained in this position. So I looked for a way out; an escape from this crazy rat race.

"How to make money online" was the exact phrase I entered into Google.

From 100+ million results, I bought countless ebooks, webinars, home study courses, membership sites and more. All using money I didn't have... My credit card bills were piling up and from all the guides I picked up one common message.

Market a product based on something you love to do.

At that time, there was something I loved. But it wasn't very appealing. It was "World of Warcraft." A computer game that I had spent over 2,300 hours playing, and the main reason why I had nearly failed college.

My first sales page was ridiculously ugly. I wrote a 32 paged ebook on how to excel at the game and slapped on a $7 price tag. Awesome! And so I waited for the sales to roll in.

Nothing happened. For seven full months.

Then one morning, as I was preparing to head for work, I got an email. It said: Notification of Payment Received.

It was from Paypal. For $7. It was at that moment that I believed that this whole thing... making money online... was real.

I scaled up the process, improved on the guide, bumped it up to $37 and realized that it sold even better when the price was higher. Four months later, I was consistently making 2-4 sales at $37 a day.

And then something unusual happened. One morning, my inbox was literally spammed by Paypal notifications. I tallied up the sales, there was a total of 512 units sold... Which added up to a total of $19,129.

I had never seen that kind of money my entire life. And I had made it, overnight, while I slept. What had happened was that one of the "big boys" in the World of Warcraft niche, sent an email out promoting my guide, which paid a 50% commission for every sale made.

One email. For nearly ten large. That's more than some CEOs make in a month.

That's email marketing. Something we'll be talking about later in this book. That moment changed my life. I started writing more guides, diversifying within the gaming niche. Then during the social media gaming boom in 2009, I published a guide called Farmville Secrets under the pen name Tony Sanders. I didn't write a word. It was outsourced for a total of $756. It generated over $1.3 million in sales in less 8 months.

When I met John, I shared my monetization strategies with him. I showed him how to take his monetization strategies to the next level and helped him implement them to huge success. This book is our way of giving back. While John is the blogging go-to guy and will be your ultimate guide to creating a popular blog, I'm the guy that's going to teach you specific tactics that you can use to generate a 6-figure income from sharing something that you love.

The Formula for Success

Blogging Secrets is not just about blogging. It is about creating a website that embodies your passions and displays to the world what you want most from and for your business. It is about creating a platform that will succeed no matter what happens to the Internet, because you are the commodity and you will never lose value.

Most of all it is about setting goals and doing whatever it takes to achieve those goals and find success online - even when millions of others can't quite figure it out.

With a blog you can do almost anything and you can have a blast doing it. So, enjoy and read carefully - don't skip anything or ignore the advice I give unless you've tried it at least once.

I've been doing this for a long time and I can assure you that success is out there waiting to be earned - you just need the right platform from which to search.

Chapter One:
Blogging - It Builds Bank Accounts

Blogging is my bread and butter. I've been doing it for years, and in that time I've been lucky enough to grow my audience to unprecedented levels and generate countless thousands of daily readers.

To a lot of people this is amazing. Heck, to me it's amazing a lot of the time.

So, when I sit down and have conversations with reporters or when someone finds my site for the first time and wants to know more about what I do, the first question I often get is "how do you make money?"

Industry professionals and readers alike are dumbfounded that a guy with a laptop and a simple Wordpress blog can pull in five figures a month from that blog. I'm not quite ready to show you my secret sauce for monetizing a blog, but I want to show you a little bit about what my blog has done and why I have this conversation so often.

That's me and this is my blog.

I write a handful of posts every month and then spend the rest of my time promoting the content I just wrote and building a larger audience.

By following the strategies I've outlined for you in the following chapters, I now make over $40,000 a month from my blog. It comes from a variety of income streams, but the most important thing you need to know right now is that it really is just a blog.

I'm not selling books. I'm not selling coaching programs. I'm not asking for donations or running a pyramid scheme in the proverbial "back office" of the web. I'm just writing killer content and making sure as many people as possible see it.

So, how does blogging build bank accounts and, more importantly, why should you consider building one if you are eager to build a business online?

Here is my philosophy on web-marketing.

The point of it, when you strip away the chaff and the glitter and the popovers and really look at what we are doing, is to provide value to our readers. People *need* something and to fulfill that need, they will turn to whomever they can trust most.

Unfortunately, the Internet is loaded with shills and charlatans - men and women who will do and say just about anything to make a buck. Faceless, sometimes nameless, and full of promises, these guys will do whatever they can to get as many people as possible to buy whatever they are selling.

I know because I get emails all the time from people warning me about the next big scam or asking me if I think a recent launch is legitimate.

What does this have to do with blogging?

Everything.

Consider what a blog really is. It's a platform on which an individual (let's say me) shares personal stories, recommendations, and insights about a specific industry or niche. And it goes beyond just sharing - it's a two way street. A blog allows me to encourage my readers to ask questions, call me out when they think I'm off base or present their side of the story.

It's a conversation that I happen to be leading, and over time that conversation has made me into something of a leader in my field.

When people see my name, they trust it. They trust that I will say and do things that are beneficial to them because, over the course of the last 7 years, I've shown time and again that that's my goal. To help people.

Now, compare that to the glut of crap out there - the 24 hour squeeze pages or the "launches" that are full of the same tired junk but at five times the cost.

Maybe you're starting to see why blogging is such a powerful medium.

A blog is a brand-building juggernaut. When done properly (I'll soon show you how), a blog allows you to create thousands of personal relationships with people who will trust your recommendations, read your posts religiously and even, yes, buy your products when you start to release them.

What a Blog Really Does

Between 2009 and 2011, the number of major corporations that have blogs grew by 50%. At the same time, in 2010, it was found that only 11% of Fortune 100 companies had actually updated their blogs in the previous three months. In short, there are a lot of people out there trying to use blogs and failing.

The reason is simple. A blog is not a press release platform. It's not a personal journal. It's not even a column in a paper. It's a blog - there is no immediate correlation between blogging and old media - it's too different and offers too many opportunities (and potential pitfalls) to be anything but.

The one thing all those flailing corporate blogs have in common is a lack of focus and vision. There is this misconception floating around that a blog is meant to be informal, relaxed and updated when "you have something to say".

That's all fine and good if you're blogging about your upcoming wedding or tricks your Schnauzer did last week. But, if you want your blog to be successful (as in cash in your pocket, successful), then it needs to be treated like any other business endeavor.

I'm going to avoid jargon and wishy-washy language in this book as much as possible - it's confusing and more often than not, it buries the point, so I'll be blunt.

You need a plan. Here's what that entails:

1. **What's Your Purpose?** - Ask yourself early and often what the goal of your site is and what you hope to get out of it. I hope that your goal is not

ONLY to make money. That is certainly a nice trade off, but a good blog comes from a place of passion in your heart, meaning you truly and honestly enjoy what you are doing. Money alone won't fill that space. You need a real purpose which will define how your site is built.

2. **Listening 101** - You need to listen to people in your niche, on other blogs and in other circles in your field. This includes forums, comments on your blog, posts on other blogs and respected news sources. Are you listening to the people in your niche that define what is interesting right now? If not, you should be.

3. **Be a Person** - Blogs are run by people, not ideas. You need to show your full personality in everything you write or record and build the blog around that as much as or more than the content itself. Good content can carry a blog, but only a strong personality will make it a success.

4. **Create Content** - Finally, it's time to create content. You need to have a plan in place for what types of content you will create, when you will create it and how you will revise and reform your content plan over time based on the results you see in Analytics and in the feedback you receive.

We're going to go much more in-depth on all four of these elements in the coming chapters, but for now I want you to start thinking about how they apply to your blog. How can you start outlining a purpose for your blog? What type of content can you create and how will it play to your ideal audience? What persona do you want to present to your readers? (hopefully, it's your persona).

Answer these questions and you will immediately be *that much closer* to having a killer blog that actually works as intended.

The Great Content Boom of 2011

Someone asked me the other day how screwed I was because of the Google Panda update. I told them "not at all" and they were dumbfounded. I write about Internet marketing and have a boat load of ads on my site. How was I not dinged?

I've written about this a handful of times before, but I want to really get down to the root of the issue because a lot of people either misunderstand Panda and Google's other content-related algorithm updates (like Caffeine and Penguin) or they don't realize any of them exist at all (possibly an even bigger problem).

Here's what Google did in 2011 when they launched Panda, from the words of Matt Cutts, Google's head of search spam:

Improve the quality of content or if there is some part of your site that has got especially low-quality content, or stuff that really not all that useful, then it might make sense to not have that content on your site.

It's all about quality.

I've seen lengthy posts about this as people try to parse the language, figure out exactly how Google analyzes and determines quality issues and what they are actively working on in their next updates, but who cares. The answer is simple, and if you don't think it is, you probably have been cheating a little.

Google wants quality for its users, and their algorithm updates (which are 100% automated by the way) are designed to ensure quality search engine

19

results. All that's happened is that Google has figured out ways to teach its spiders how to see if a page of content is actually any good.

In the past Google measured a lot of technical details - things like incoming backlinks, anchor text, site structure and navigation. That stuff all still matters, but Google is looking for things like originality, time spent on the page by your readers, and actual quality of writing and giving those elements much more weight.

So, while you can certainly read until your eyes bleed about their updates, Google is telling us (practically screaming, really) what they want. And that's quality content.

This is good news for people like me because I always focused on the user experience above and beyond all else in developing my blog. When I created the blog, I wanted to write content that my readers could use and that reflected my personal experiences online. So, I have and still do spend hours researching, writing and publishing posts, and I actively engage with each of my readers to ensure the site is as value-packed as possible.

And because I provide just what Google is looking for, my site wasn't touched by those algorithm updates - still hasn't been.

I'll talk a lot more in future chapters about what it means to create really killer content and to generate the stuff other people are looking for. But right now, all you really need to know is that content gets the job done and you already have the tools to make that content - don't over think it.

What to Write About

Another big question I get about blogging is what someone should write about. Inevitably, this question comes in one of two forms - either A) what topic is the most profitable and B) can I write about the same stuff as you?

In both cases, the questioner is missing the point. They are seeing me sitting at my laptop, making 7 figures a year with a blog and thinking "damn, I want to do that and I'll write about anything that can get those kinds of numbers."

This is the *wrong* path.

My blog is successful because I am passionate about what I write, research and record. I love my work and I love sharing my insights and experiences with other people. But if this niche suddenly lost all income potential and I was eager to start a new blog, I wouldn't write about dog training just because someone told me there was money to be made in it.

I don't know a thing about training dogs and I certainly don't want to try and pretend I do when there are millions of people better suited to write on the topic. I won't be successful, and even if I am, it wouldn't be genuine.

Your blog needs to be a reflection of your passions. The last thing you should think about is monetization when you're picking your topic. That will come in time, and with very few exceptions, almost any type of blog can be made profitable.

The big question then is not "what is a profitable niche" but "what niche I can write about every day".

Remember, for your blog to be successful, you need to be active on it *constantly*. Imagine trying to write about dog training for five days a week if you don't know anything about it. Now, imagine trying to look excited about it on video - I shudder at the thought.

A blog is a reflection of you, and if you are excited about what you write and record, other people will be just as excited. And THAT is where the profit comes in. Not by selecting a killer topic, but by writing about what you know.

So, I'm not going to tell you what to build your blog around. Instead, I will show you a handful of resources that I have used to generate topics and that I have recommended to other people in the past.

Amazon.com

No doubt you've seen this before, either on a blog (possibly mine) or in a "how to make money online" book. It's common advice, but for good reason - Amazon is an immensely powerful market research tool.

What Amazon allows you to do is search for essentially anything you could possibly be interested in and see immediately the kind of consumer response it has. Here is what I recommend.

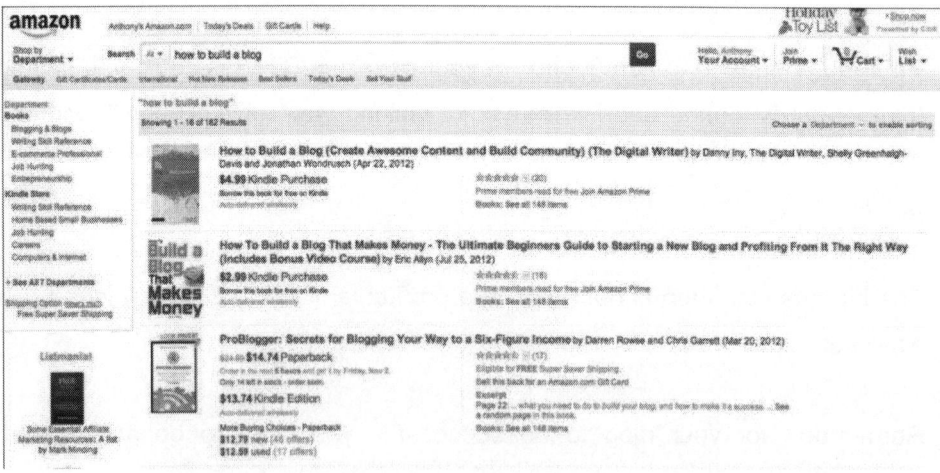

Search for a topic on Amazon, in this case I have selected "how to build a blog".

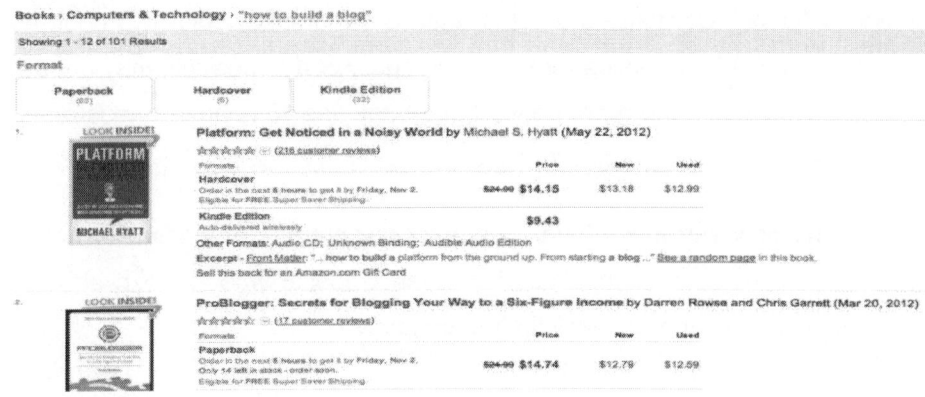

Sort the results by their popularity as this will put the top selling products toward the top of the list. Now, click on three or four of those options and look at the following details:

Product Details

Hardcover: 288 pages
Publisher: Thomas Nelson (May 22, 2012)
Language: English
ISBN-10: 159555503X
ISBN-13: 978-1595555038
Product Dimensions: 5.8 x 1.2 x 8.4 inches
Shipping Weight: 14.9 ounces (View shipping rates and policies)
Average Customer Review: ★★★★★ ☑ (216 customer reviews)
Amazon Best Sellers Rank: #4,142 in Books (See Top 100 in Books)
    #6 in Books > Computers & Technology > Web Development > **Web 2.0**
    #10 in Books > Business & Investing > Marketing & Sales > Marketing > **Web Marketing**
    #15 in Books > Business & Investing > Industries & Professions > **E-commerce**

Would you like to **update product info, give feedback on images,** or **tell us about a lower price**?

1. **Number of Reviews** - On average, for every 100-1000 (I find that it's closer to 1,000) sales, a product will get one review. So, if a product has 10 reviews, it has between 1,000 and 10,000 sales. Those books with 1,000+ reviews likely have sold close to a million copies.

2. **Sales Rank** - Compare the sales rank to the number sold. If a book has zero reviews but has a sales rank in its category of #3, then this may not be a very large niche. On the other hand, if that book has 15 reviews and is ranked #103, then this niche is very extensive

3. **Number of Written Reviews** - Look for the number of written reviews as well. This indicates a strong customer base - people who are excited about the product and willing to share their experiences.

4. **Forum Posts** - Finally, look at the very bottom for the "forum posts" section. This is where people can discuss this product or related products in similar forums. Not many products drive this kind of discussion, but if yours does, you are set.

Remember too that you don't need to look only for books. This works equally well for home products, food items and anything else you might search for on Amazon.

Other Research Tools

There are a few other tools you can use to test your topic to ensure it has a viable audience. Here are a few of them:

Google Trends

I love Google's collection of research tools because they are simple, and often these tools can give you all the information you need to get started writing. Sure, there are much more powerful research and insight tools out there, but the average blogger doesn't need stuff like that.

We have Google Trends.

Google Trends is basically a hot list of recent searches. You can search for a keyword and Google Trends will show you how it has trended since it first showed up in the index, whenever that might have been. Here's an example for my name:

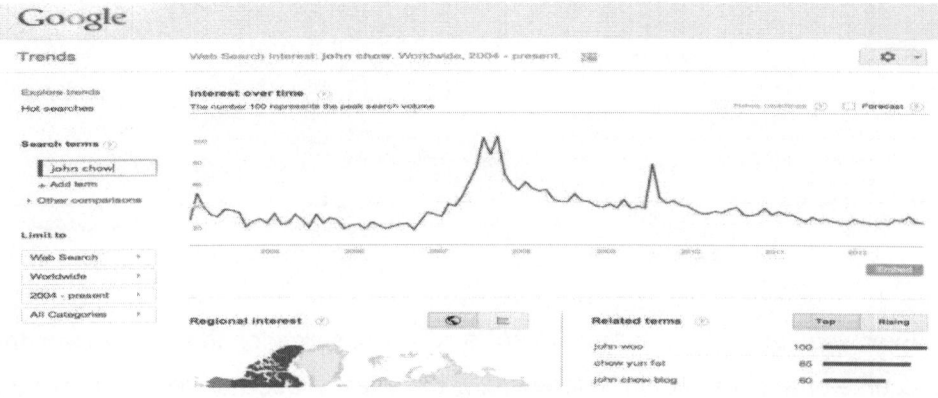

While it is certainly the case that my name is common enough around the globe, a lot of that traffic is for me. You can tell because of where it comes from - largely English speaking countries like the US and Canada. I've been trending well for some time now with some good peaks in early 2008 and mid-2009 but no clear drop-off.

That's cool to see, but the real value of a tool like Google Trends is finding things you don't already know are trending so you can write about them now.

Here's what I mean. Let's say you run a blog that covers dog shows around the world. There are probably big lists of those shows, but you can see exactly when people start to search for those new dog shows by searching for them in trend searches. For example, here is the trending pattern for the Westminster Dog Show:

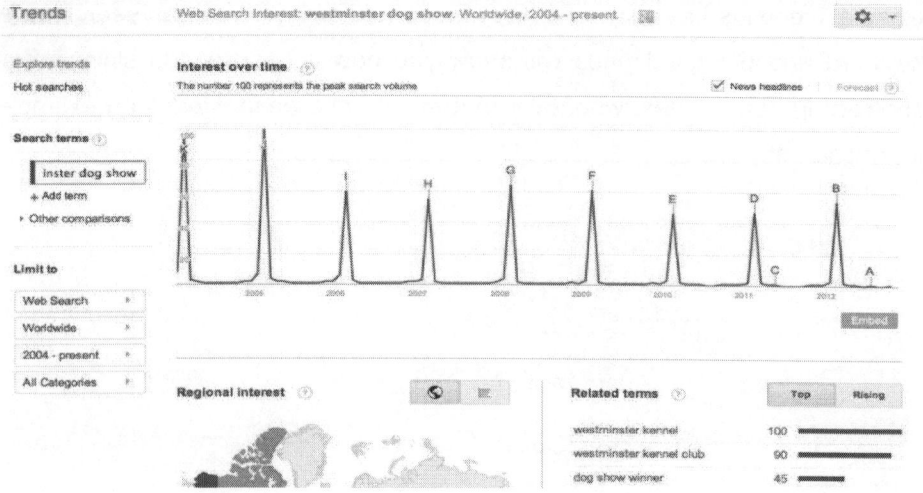

Ever year at the same time there is a sharp spike for that show over the course of about a month. Interestingly, the interest declines almost as fast as it increases, so you know that news after the show may not be that interesting - just immediately before and immediately afterwards.

You can use this to do a lot of things, but keep in mind that one of the tools used by Google to track these trends is news headlines as well as searches. That means that if you are searching for terms that are not necessarily directly written about in major news sources, they may not trend like you'd expect. For the most part, though, you'll get a very good idea of the trending patterns for a product or topic by using this tool.

What's Hot Right Now?

While in Google's Trends tool, click on "Hot Searches" and you will be given access to a list of recent hot searches, usually based around current events. A quick look through this list each day can give you topic ideas and help you tap into huge surges of traffic (assuming they relate to your blog's topics).

26

I am writing this section shortly after Hurricane Sandy in New York, so that, along with the new Star Wars movie make a big showing in the results. Of course, you can adjust or select where the hot searches are coming from to focus on other regions like India or Japan where the function has been enabled.

Here is an example from Japan:

If you don't speak Japanese, it may not make sense to you, but you can see that those topics are getting tens of thousands of searches *per day* in that region. If you wrote in Japanese you'd want to tap into that search volume.

Anyways, enough about Japan - I know my audience and I imagine a very small percentage of you will be tracking trends in other languages.

What matters is that you can see in real time what is tracking in Google and then post content that matches that tracking.

Keep in mind too that whatever you search for with the Google Keyword Tool in AdWords can be reviewed in Google Trends to see how that keyword has performed over time:

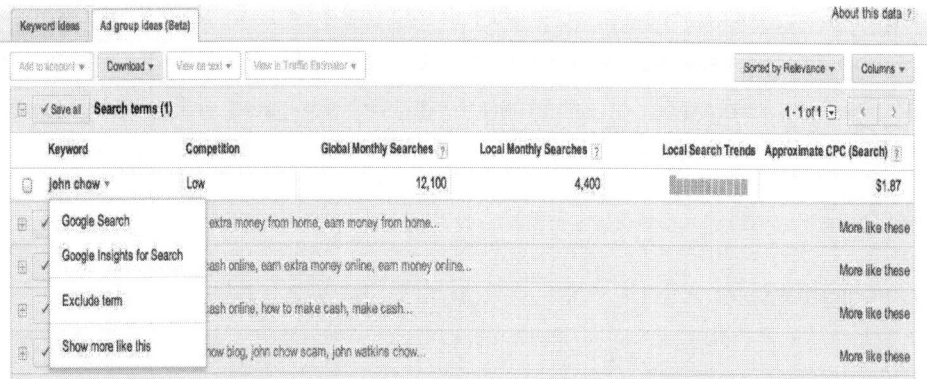

Pretty cool, eh:

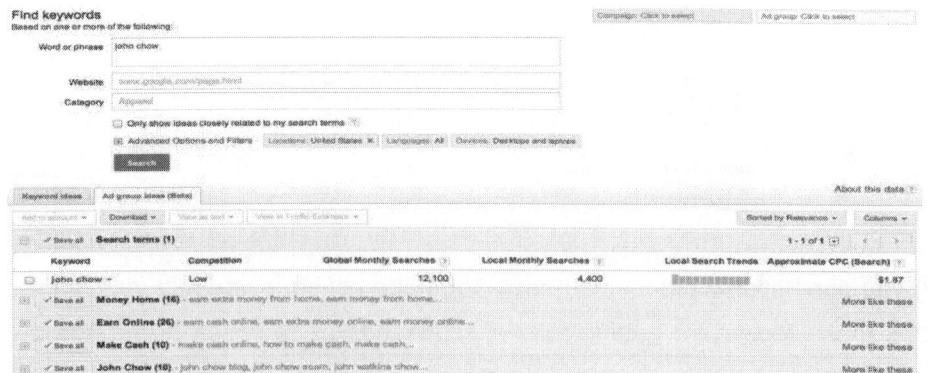

Limits to Trend Matching

This is a sort of disclaimer - before you start writing about whatever trends each day, make sure it matches your site's topics. Not only can Google sense when you are whoring out your posts for keyword love, but your readers will be annoyed if your posts are all over the place in an attempt to constantly tap the zeitgeist. Unless you're the Huffington Post you won't get away with it.

Facebook and Twitter

Google is still the far and away leader in search and indexing online, but increasingly people express their interests online through social media. If you were in the US for any of the election cycle, you remember that with each debate we got data on how many tweets were sent and what memes were started by people's statements.

It's not surprising then that these services make fantastic research tools when you're looking for blogging topics or post topics. I go into this a little more in detail later, but for now, here are some simple ways to research Facebook and Twitter for recent trends:

When it comes to Twitter, there are quite literally dozens of sites that provide instant tracking of specific terms in Twitter's constantly updating index. However, there are a few that are more powerful than others, simply because they allow you to track other services as well. One such service is Klout.

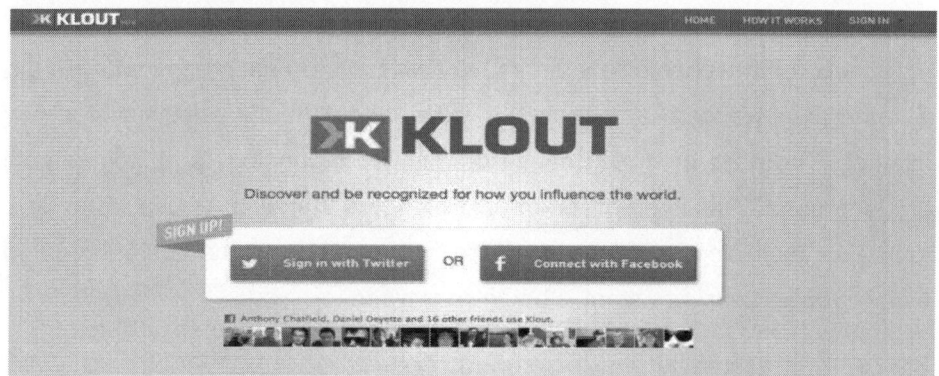

Klout is cool because it gives you a score based on the impact of your links, recommendations and opinions on sites like Twitter and Facebook (among others). It essentially goes out and measures how effectively you engage with people on ALL social media sites and then provides an aggregated score for them all, comparing you to other influencers in your niche.

Cool, eh?

There are others too if you only want to monitor things through Twitter. For example, sites like Twazzup, Twitscoop, TweetBuzzer and Monitter allow you to see in real time what is being searched for in Twitter (you define what to track of course) and what, if any of it, relates to you and your niche.

This kind of stuff is really most powerful for people who are trying to find new customers or connections through Twitter, but it can be equally powerful for someone like you that needs to see what people are talking about within a niche.

For Facebook you have fewer options, if only because actively monitoring Facebook is much tougher. There are tools, of course, but most of them cost money or are designed for parental monitoring, so it's easier in most cases to do it manually.

YouTube
Video recording technology is dirt cheap these days. That means you can get a camera or webcam and record a video about nearly anything in a few minutes. The days of limited bandwidth, limited technology and limited tools are long gone. This is great for intrepid bloggers that want to use video as a format for their blogs. At the same time, you can use all the content created by everyone else to see what is hot in your niche.

A quick search in YouTube for hot topics in your niche, especially after you've done some preliminary research in Facebook or Twitter, can go a long way toward ensuring what you write or record for your blog is what people want. Here's what I mean:

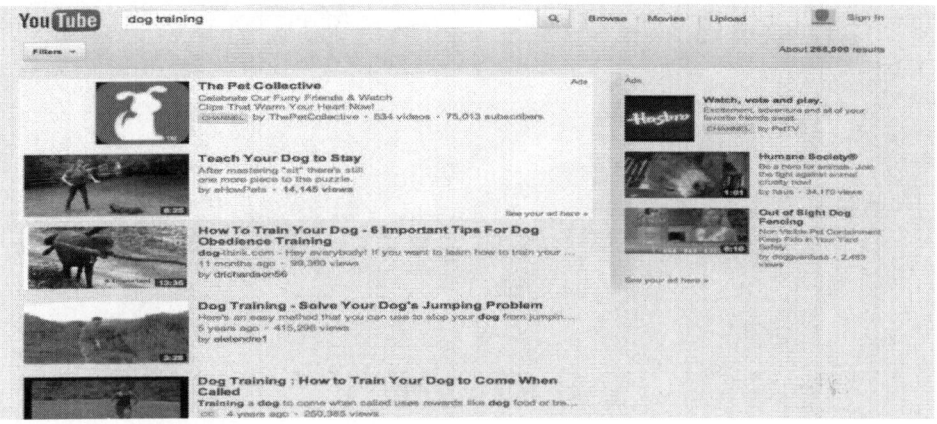

This is a simple search in YouTube for a topic in the dog training niche.

After sorting through a few pages I find that the majority of the results are like this:

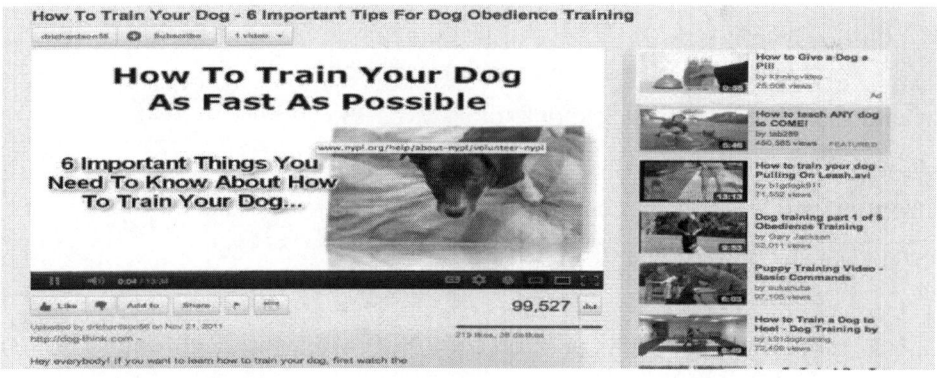

People really want this type of content, as can be seen by the number of videos like this as well as the volume of comments, likes and responses they seem to be generating. So, if you're writing in this niche and are looking for

31

topics, a great place to look for content ideas will be in YouTube and in these types of videos.

The same can be said for your actual videos. A lot of bloggers make a solid living by creating responses to other videos. They create a video that discusses a hot topic in their niche in response to another video on the same topic.

That's me giving a tour of the Affiliate Summit East in 2012 out in New York. Very simple and quick response and minimal research needed because I'm just giving my point of view on a topic.

Clickbank or Commission Junction

You won't find a lot of blog ideas necessarily on Commission Junction, Clickbank or any of the other affiliate networks, but you will get a clear idea of what products convert well and which ones are being promoted most heavily.

Let's take a quick look at Clickbank for an example.

This is a search for "dog training". As you can

see, there are a lot of products with fairly high gravity for this topic. The top rated products are those that have a "high gravity", or in other words, a large number of affiliates successfully selling that product.

While this is not necessarily a direct reflection of the interest of your audience, it does show that there are quite a few people out there buying that product, and therefore a lot of people promoting it. It also means that, if you wrote a blog about dog training, the audience would probably be large enough to support your efforts.

The same goes with Commission Junction, though in a slightly different way.

Most stuff on Clickbank is a product, often independent of a brand. Those authors are usually pseudonyms and the really big products are often sold through major launches in the IM niche. Commission Junction and other CPA networks have a lot of different offers, many of which are branded.

So the data here can be misleading. People promote those brands because they match their audiences, not the other way around. And of course, a lot of the higher ranking ones are in high payout niches like insurance - so don't necessarily be discouraged if your niche isn't blowing it up on CPA networks.

Take gaming for example. If you searched for gaming products (one of Peng Joon's big niches) on Commission Junction, you wouldn't find many. But here are the gravity results on Clickbank:

Blowing up the results here.

33

The goal in all of this again is not to monetize before you start writing, but to ensure that whatever you write will have an eager audience when it gets out there. If you are interested in writing about a newer topic or something that is still developing, these strategies may not be necessary as you're speculating to a certain degree. But it can still help to get the pulse on what people want or need in that niche.

Your Brand

A blog is a brand. It's a direct reflection of you and what you think about a given topic or set of topics.

Your brand needs to be unique and fully fleshed out if you want it to stand out among your competitors, and yes, you will have competitors. So, before you start writing, answer the following questions:

* **Who will read what you write?** - Create a short outline of the ideal reader for your blog. Who do you want reading your content and what will they get out of it. I guarantee that your eventual audience will surprise you and you will likely change your site more than a couple times as you uncover some really interesting data based on the searches you get, but this is a good place to start.

* **Who are your contemporaries?** - You can learn more about your potential readers by looking at potential competitor blogs - the blogs of people who write about what you want to write about. Check the comments, review the content and its style, and interact with the author and their readers.

* **What personal experiences do you bring to the site?** - Your job is not just to write how-to content or report the news. If that's all you do you'll never create a viable blog. You need to have stories. You are a storyteller and that

means creating a site that is engaging to people because of *you* not the content you share.

* **Are you unique in any specific way?** - Write down every way that you are unique from your competitors. This includes your world experiences, your writing style, your opinions on things, and even the type of content you will create.

* **What do people like most about your existing content?** - If you've written anything to date, either for a blog or just for the hell of it, what do people like most about it? What specific things do they point to and say "hey, that's pretty good"? Now, do it again.

The goal is not just to outline your blog (though that can certainly help), but to ensure that whatever you do write is unique. Too many bloggers churn out five or six posts a week that are nothing more than copy-paste jobs of existing blog posts on competitor sites. They rewrite the content to pass Google's muster, but they fail to bring anything new and exciting to that field.

Assume that your readers are also reading all of the other blogs in your niche. Now, what can you write that will encourage those readers to visit your site *first*? That's the difference between writing and branding.

Chapter Two:
Launching Your Blog

I'm going to assume, just to ensure that everyone is on the same page, that you have not yet created your blog. If you have and you're eager to start writing, feel free to jump to Chapter 4 in which I will talk about creating your brand, building your site and writing your first posts.

But even if you have built a blog already, I encourage you to read through this chapter and make sure you're taking full advantage of all the tools that are out there for your site.

For everyone else, this is required reading. Too often I see bloggers wing this part of it - just putting something out there and writing - without a base in place to support their growing endeavor. The best way to really be successful as a blogger is not just to write content for that blog, but to ensure it matches the specific needs of your readers. And that means you need a good platform in place before you write anything.

Blog Software Galore

This is the part where most books throw a list of 5-10 different types of blog software at you with pros and cons for each. Let's skip that because, honestly, there really is only one you should be using. Wordpress.

Wordpress is the most powerful, flexible, and ultimately effective blogging software available, and it's free so there is no reason *not* to use it.

The only big question you'll need to ask up front is whether you want a free Wordpress.com blog or would like to build a Wordpress.org blog on your own domain name.

The former is 100% free and can always be transferred to the latter fairly easily, while the Wordpress.org option will cost you at least $15 up front for a domain name and $5/month for hosting. I strongly recommend the second option if you can afford it, but if you can't, a Wordpress.com blog is a good place to start (and the following tutorials will still apply).

So, what is so great about Wordpress?

To start, it's open source, which means that anyone can add content to it as they see fit. You can install plugins or new widgets or you can have someone perform some custom coding to create segments you like. There are thousands of themes available, both free and paid, that can make your blog look like a professional corporate blog or an exact clone of those old Blogger sites.

You can do essentially anything you want with Wordpress, and with so many plugins and tools at your disposal, you can leverage even small efforts into big traffic gains.

Creating Your Wordpress Blog

If you want to create a Wordpress.com site, it's as simple as going to Wordpress.com, creating an account and setting up your first blog (the site will walk you through these steps). Wordpress.org sites are a little more complicated, but not much.

Here are the steps involved in creating your new Wordpress site.

1. Buy a Domain Name

To buy a domain name, go to a site like Namecheap.com or GoDaddy.com and do a quick search for whatever you want your domain name to be. I used my name, which made my life considerably easier and allowed me to do some extensive branding as I built up my business.

You don't have to do the same though, especially if you have a relatively common name and it is not available to register. One thing to keep in mind, though, is that your domain name should be matched to your niche, and it should be less than 15 characters if possible. It should also be a dotcom domain name (avoid those new options like .info, .mobi, and .co).

Other than that, go to town and choose whatever you think will best match your personality and the content you plan on building for your site.

2. Choose a Hosting Plan

Next, you need a hosting plan. This is the server on which your website will be stored, so it is important you choose one that is both reliable and scalable. There are thousands of webhosts out there, but I have always recommended and still do recommend HostGator.

They offer very low cost introductory plans (just $5/month), and you can easily upgrade your account whenever your traffic increases to the point that you need more bandwidth. So why not buy a domain name with the same company you choose for hosting or use GoDaddy or Namecheap as your host? I have long recommended keeping the two separate. If you ever want to move your host (companies go downhill all the time), it's a much bigger pain in the backside if you purchased your domain name from them directly.

3. Install Wordpress

One of the big benefits of choosing HostGator's shared hosting is that you can install WordPress in three clicks. Here's how it works:

Step 1: Go to your domain's Control Panel. For example, assume I've bought the domain www.buyacar.com

To login into my domain's Control Panel, I need to type this URL in my internet browser: www.buyacar.com/cpanel. In other words, you need to enter your domain followed by "/cpanel/".

Step 2: Enter your username and password (which can be found in the email from sales@hostgator.com that was sent to you when you purchased a server at HostGator).

Press the login button and you should see your domain's control panel which looks like this:

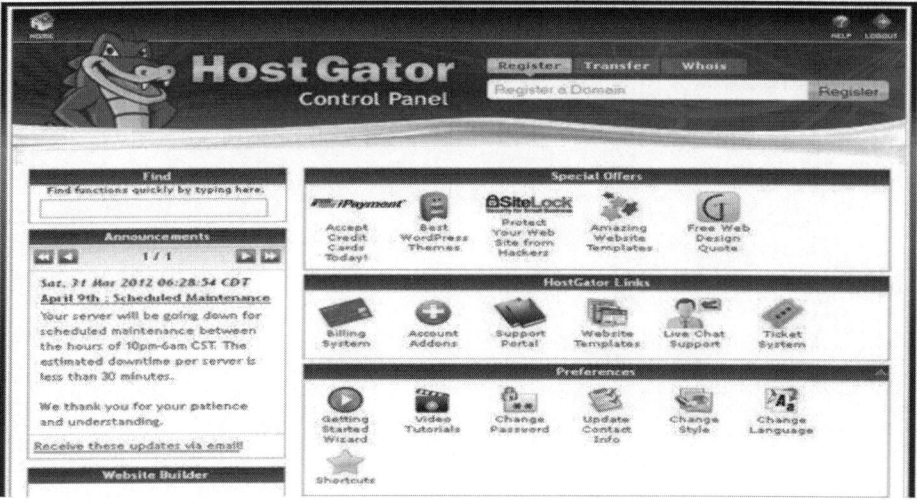

39

Step 3: Scroll down to the "Software/Services" section and click on the smiley button that reads "Fantastico De Luxe".

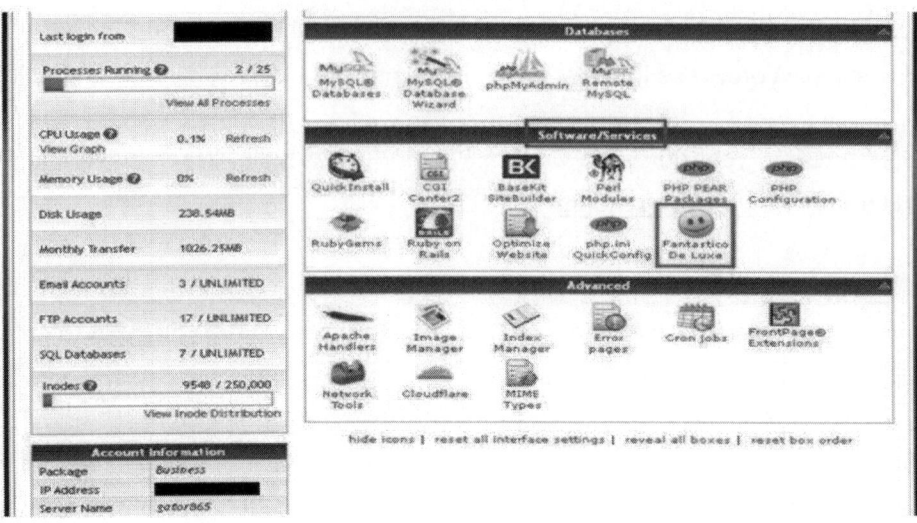

Step 4: Click on "Wordpress".

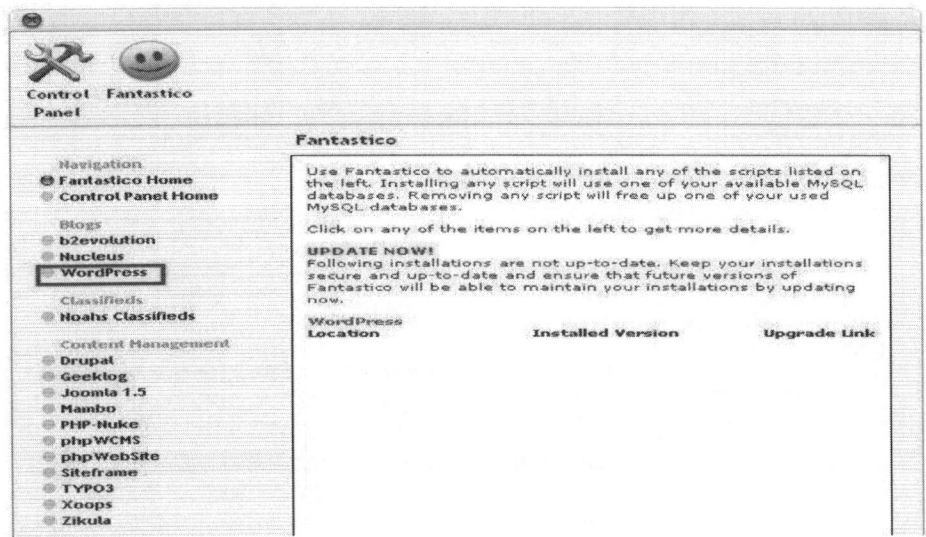

Step 5: Select "New Installation".

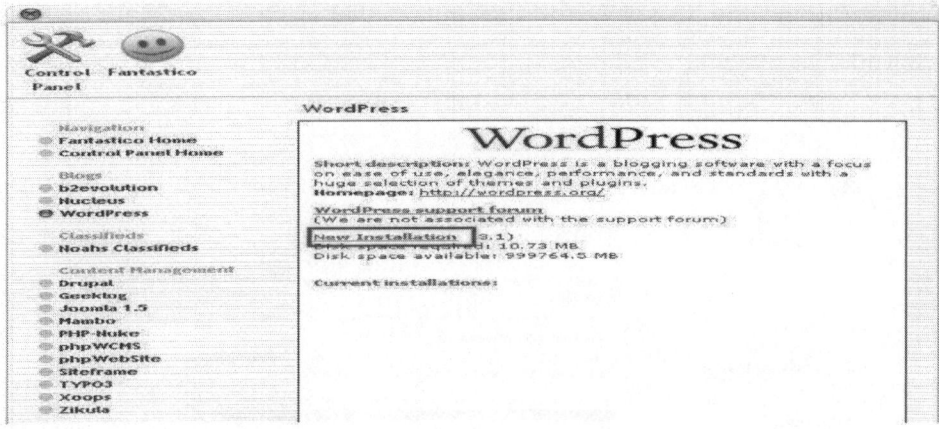

Step 6: You should have only one domain on your server right now - the one you purchased earlier from Namecheap. (Red Arrow pointing towards the domain that you have).

Leave the "Install in Directory" blank.

Enter the admin access data details that you choose and please write them down. For this example, I have entered:Login: admin (same as admin nickname) Password: passwordAdmin. email: support@buyacar.com

41

Step 7: Press the "Install WordPress" button after filling in the details and you will see this screen:

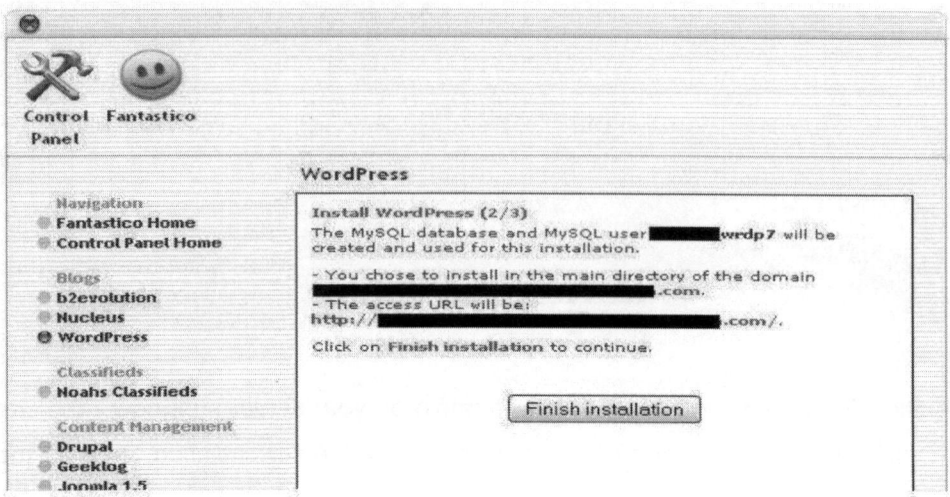

Click the "Finish Install" button.

Step 8: You will see the screen that signifies successful installation. Press the red "x" mark on the top left of the screen and log out.

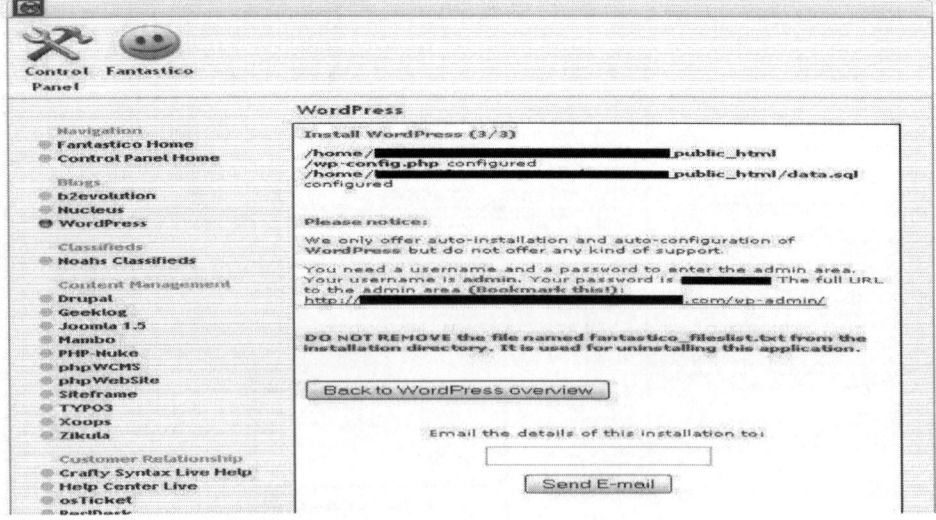

Step 9: It's done! Visit your domain and this is what you will see on your website.

That's it – the quick install method works with any HostGator account and can be replicated on other sites if you ever create more sites on the same account. As you can see it's very easy and doesn't require any technical knowledge to set up.

Setup WordPress

Now that WordPress is installed, you can login using the username and password you provided and start blogging. There are a lot of aesthetic upgrades you can and should make to avoid your site looking like this:

43

But for all intents and purposes, you can start blogging today if you have something to say. And keep in mind that any aesthetic changes you make later will be applied to your existing blog posts, so there is no good reason *not* to start writing now if you're ready.

That's it. You're ready to start blogging right away. However, if you're interested in customizing your blog further and making it look like you've always envisioned, keep reading for some more tips.

A Quick Tour of the WordPress Backend

I have a lot of videos and content on my site that will walk you through how WordPress works and what you can get out of it.

But, I still want to take a few moments and show you the core stuff you'll need to know how to use in WordPress when creating new posts. This is not meant to be comprehensive as there are a lot of resources out there on this topic – I just want to ensure you know what you need to get started today:

The Walkthrough

Let's take a quick look at the WordPress dashboard.

This is what you see when you login to WordPress for the first time. On the left side of the screen you will see this:

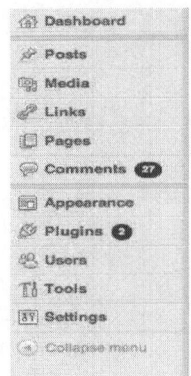

What you'll see there is a long list of options, including anything you've installed from your plugins list. Here are the ones you need to know about right away:

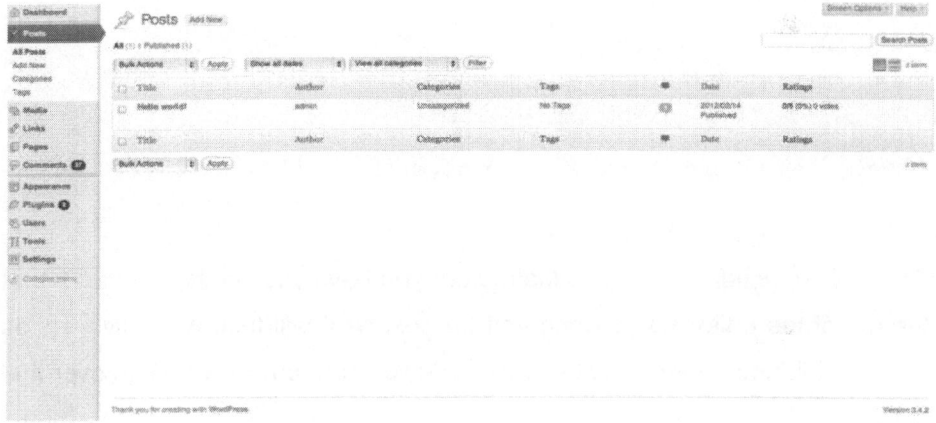

Posts

When you click on Posts you will see all of the posts that you have written to date, along with a link to "add new" posts to your blog. You can click on any one of the existing posts to edit it, or you can create a new one and you will see the following:

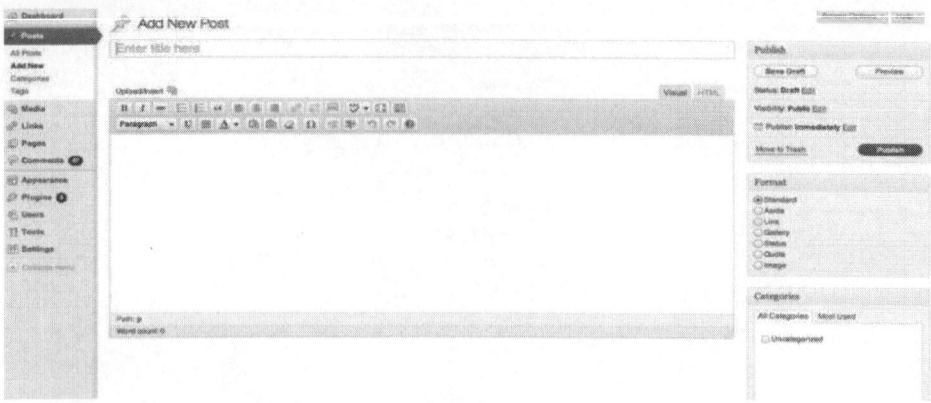

On this screen, you have a lot of options, but to write a post, you need only to add a Title where it says "Enter title here" and then fill in the actual content of the post. If you've used a word processor like Word or Pages, you know exactly what to do here.

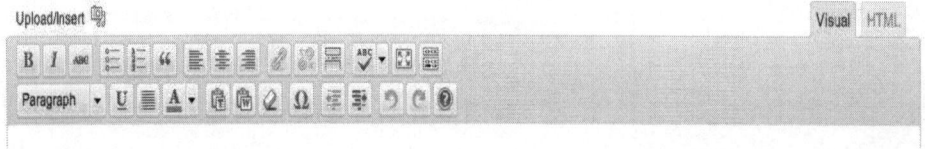

This is your visual editing bar. Make sure you have clicked the "visual" tab at the top of the editor so you can edit the text as it will look when live. If you know HTML and prefer to edit in that mode you can, but we won't go over that here.

Upload/Insert

This little icon will allow you to upload images, videos and other media to your site.

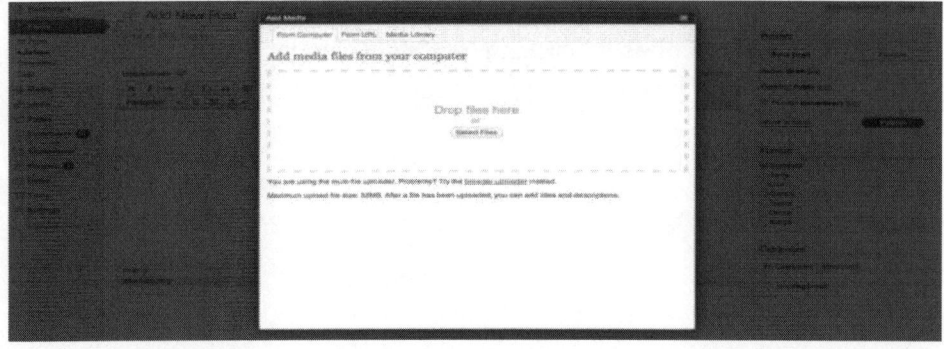

Just drag the file you want to upload into the box (or find it on your computer) and it will start to upload.

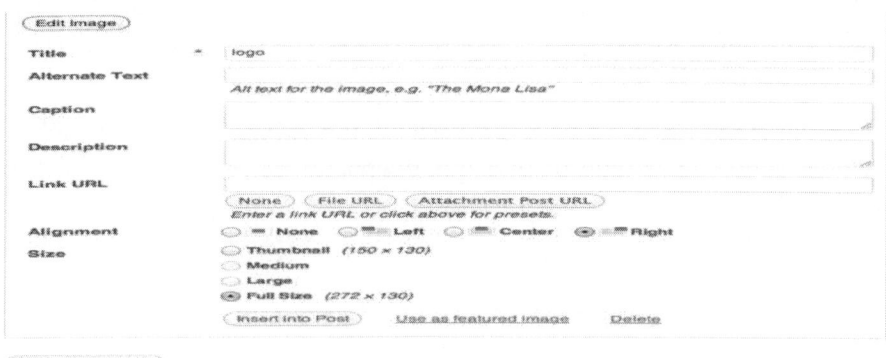

To add that file to your post, click the "insert to post" link as shown above. There are a lot of other options there you can edit including the title, caption and Alt tag, as well as the size of the image you add. Feel free to play with these as needed.

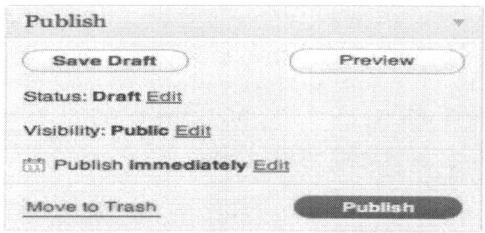

Finally, when your post is written and ready to upload, you can set the categories. Add new ones by clicking "add new category" and you can do the same for tags below this.

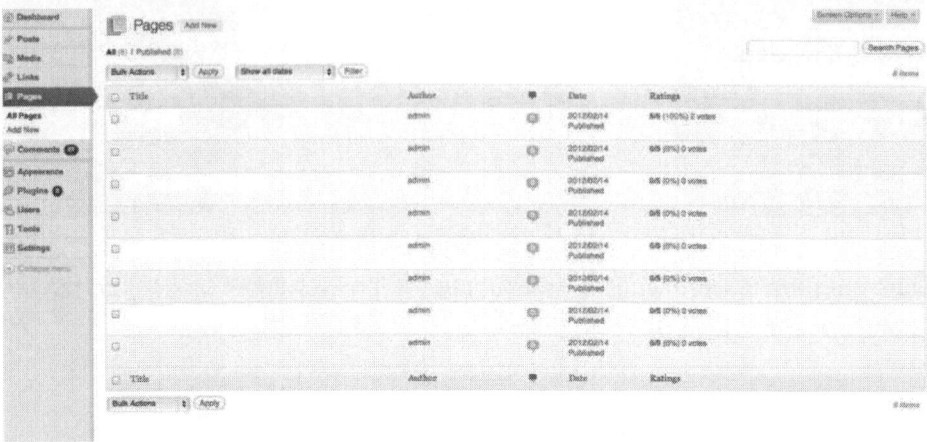

Now, either click "save draft" or "publish" if you want your post to go live immediately. You can also schedule the post to go live in the future by changing the "Publish Immediately" link to a specific date and time.

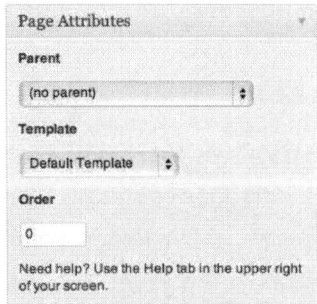

Pages

Pages are are edited and added the same way posts are, so I won't go back through that process in detail. But there are some key differences that we should go over.

As you can see, there are no categories here. Instead, if you want to create a hierarchy for pages, you would create a parent page, and then when you create a new page you would select that page as its parent.

The effect, when you change your permalinks, is that the URL will look like this:

http://www.yoursite.com/page1/page2/

If you want to get all your keywords into the page titles, this is a great way to do it. Of course, as a blogger, you are writing mostly posts and not pages, so don't get carried away with this. Pages should be used solely for permanent things that you want to appear on the home page, like your "About" page, "Contact" page and other pages in the same vein.

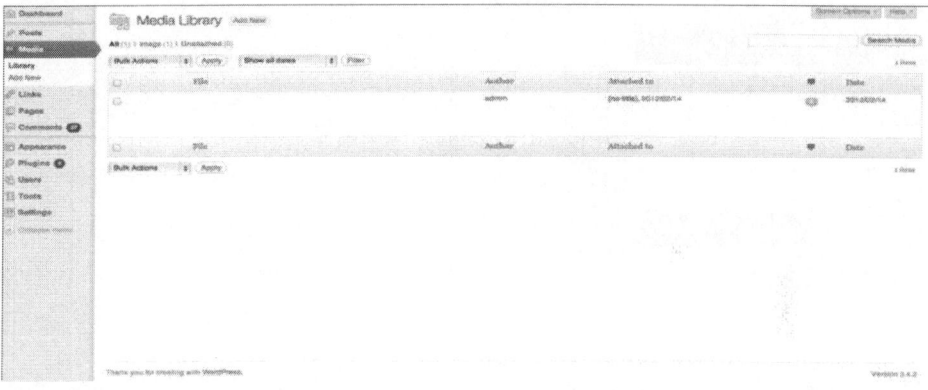

Media

You can upload and manage media directly from the media menu on the dashboard. This is a much faster way to add and change media options than by using the media shortcut inside the post editing page.

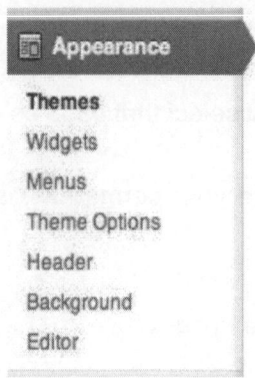

Appearance

Under the Appearance menu there are four options:

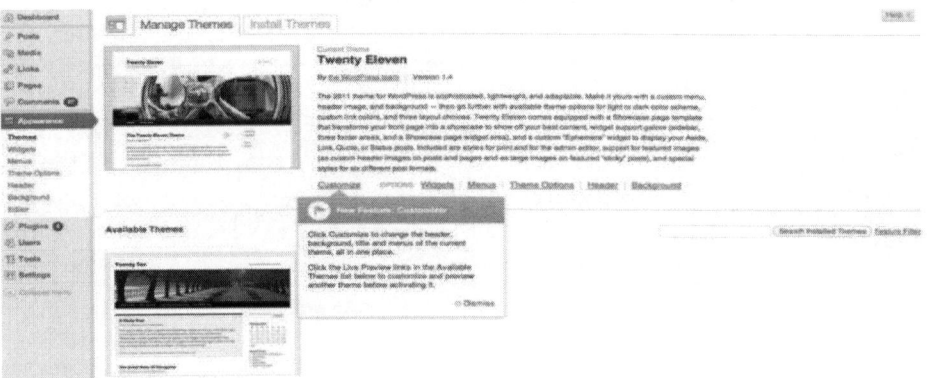

The first is to upload or change your theme. This will be useful when you want to customize the look of your WordPress blog. The second is to add or change widgets. These are the blocks of content that appear on the sidebar or in the footer of your site and the options for adjusting them will vary depending on the theme you're using.

The third option is to change menus. WordPress (and most of the themes you can purchase or download) have custom menus. This allows you to select

50

which pages or even which posts and categories appear in menus at the top of your site, along the sidebar and in the footer below your site.

Finally, there is the editing option. This allows you to actively edit the theme files for your site. I don't recommend you do this unless you know exactly what you are doing and what effect it will have on your site.

Plugins

Plugins are pieces of code that change the function of your WordPress blog or add new functions to it. I've included a list of plugins later in the book that I highly recommend you install, and there are thousands more that add extensive functionality to your site. Pretty much anything you can think to make your site do, there is a plugin for.

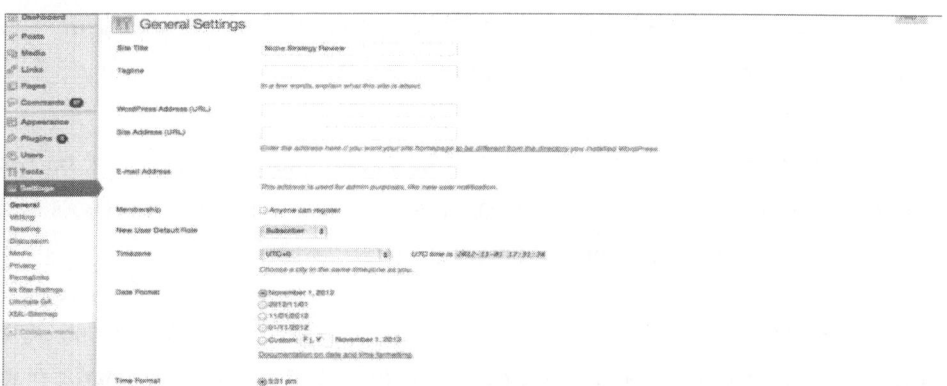

51

Settings

Finally, the settings menu. This is a big one as there are quite a few options in here you can change. They include:

1   **General** – General options include the site title and tagline, the actual URL of the site, the email address of the administrator (you), the membership setup, user default roles and time zone.

2   **Writing** – Under writing you'll find a handful of useful tools that will affect how you write new posts. Things like how big your writing box is when posting, the types of emoticons that will show up, post categories, and tools to post by button or post by email.

3   **Reading** – Reading allows you to define what will show up on your front page, the length of the blog post pages and what will show up in the RSS feed.

4   **Discussion** – This allows you to change a number of commenting options including the use of gravatars, moderation settings, when you get emailed, and other comment settings such as nesting and how long they stay in moderation.

5   **Media** – Under media you can define how thumbnails are created and stored, what embedding does in the blog, where files are uploaded and how they are organized once uploaded.

6   **Privacy** – Privacy refers almost exclusively to whether your blog will or will not appear in search results. Make sure this is turned off once your site is ready to launch or you won't get much traffic.

7   **Permalinks** – Permalinks refer to how WordPress creates and displays the URL for a given blog post. By default, it will assign a number to

each post, so your URLs will look like this: http://www.yoursite.com/p?=8935. That's not search engine friendly. So, as soon as you can, go to Permalinks and change it to custom: /%category%/%postname%. This will ensure that every link in your site includes the name of the post and the category in which it is stored.

Additionally, anything you add through a plugin or custom theme is likely to show up in here as well. So if you install a plugin and can't find its options, they are probably under "settings".

That's not all of them obviously. There are also tools for backing up or importing content to your blog, moderating comments, editing a specific theme and much more. But the options listed above will cover 90% of what you do in WordPress on any given day.

Setting Up and Customizing Your WordPress Site

Once you've installed your new WordPress site, the next step is to make sure it looks and acts like you want it to. You can always make changes in the future, but a lot of these things are good to plan out and put in place now with the expectation that your site will grow and become more popular in the future.

There are three major things to consider here – themes, plugins and graphics – so I'm going to take you through each of them one at a time and share some of my favorite options.

Themes
Like I showed you above, your WordPress site will look like this when it comes out of the package:

53

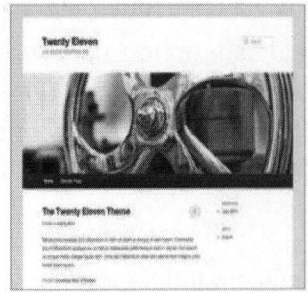
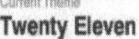
That's the twentyeleven theme and it comes by default with all WordPress.org installs. Fortunately, you can change this in just about any way you want. I'm using the exact same platform for JohnChow.com and mine looks like this:

That's a custom theme.

When it comes to themes, you essentially have two options – either free or paid themes. The free options are actually quite attractive when created by the right people. They just don't happen to get a lot of care and often lack some power features you might like to have for your site.

Pros and Cons of Free Themes

The obvious pro of a free theme is that it is free. That means you can try out as many of them as you want and they are usually fairly basic, meaning they are easy to edit and quick to install.

The problem with free themes is that they are often somewhat limited. They don't have a lot of bells and whistles, which is fine when you're just starting, but eventually you probably want something a little more powerful. Another possible issue you'll encounter when using free themes is support. If you choose a free theme, it is still best to select one from a company that offers commercial options as well like Woo Themes or Rocket Themes. This way you can be sure the theme will keep up with any new Wordpress updates, ensuring you don't have any security issues in the future.

Pros and Cons of Paid Themes

This one is easy - paid themes cost money. That's basically all there is to it. A paid theme is going to take a chunk of cash out of your pocket. It's worth it 99.9% of the time, but if you don't have that money right away, it's a tough call.

If you're on a budget, however, and would like a paid theme that looks good and reflects the core purpose of your site, here are a few theme sites to consider:

* **Woo Themes** - Woo Themes are extremely popular for good reason. While the blogs on this site are generally created with eCommerce in mind (they even have their own eCommerce plugin), they are extremely versatile and can be used in a number of settings. The cost is high, however, starting at $70 per theme (or $125 plus $25 per month for access to all themes).

* **Rocket Themes** - Rocket Themes makes content for a lot of CMS platforms and have been around for a long time. They don't have quite the same following as Woo or Elegant but they have some great looking themes starting at $50 (and a good selection of freebies)

* **Elegant Themes** - Elegant Themes are all about simplicity and good-looking design. If you want a premium theme that looks really freaking good and don't need a lot of functions to go with it, then one of these may be for you. These are only sold through a membership, which costs $40 to start.

* **Theme Forest** - Theme Forest is an a la carte marketplace where individual theme creators can post their work for other people to look through. I like Theme Forest because of its diversity, but keep in mind that some of these themes may not get updated as often.

* **Genesis Framework** - StudioPress has created one very powerful theme called Genesis which can be tweaked and revised to work in almost any setting. The core framework is free, but the child themes that they sell on their site cost $80 or more each. It's well worth it, however, if you want a powerful theme.

56

* **Thesis Theme** - Thesis is another powerful standalone theme that has multiple skins and child themes you can use to customize the layout. Thesis starts at $87 but can cost as much as $197 for the unlimited support and upgrades option. For the record, this is my favorite - it is just too powerful not to like.

There are hundreds of other sites out there too, but to me these are the big six. They have the best support, the most diverse options for upgrades and are very user friendly. Theme Forest should be treaded on gently, however, due to the support issues that can arise because the people creating these themes are often freelance developers.

Installing a Theme

Installation of a new theme is fairly easy. You can do it one of two ways. Either, download the .ZIP folder and upload it directly into WordPress or upload the files individually via an FTP client. Here's a quick look at both:

Upload the Theme File

You can search for free themes in the WordPress Codex or you can upload a file directly that you download from a paid theme site.

Manage Themes	Install Themes

Akismet is almost ready. You must enter your Akismet API key for it to work.

Search I Upload I Featured I Newest I Recently Updated

Search for themes by keyword.

[   ] (Search)

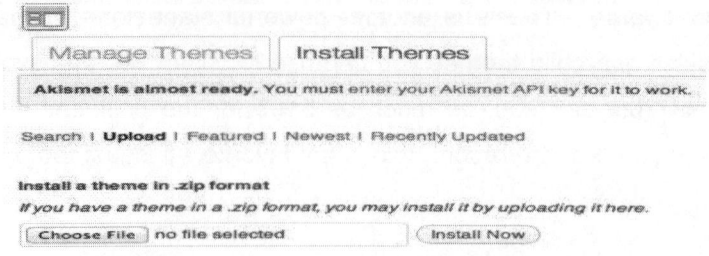

If you are uploading a file, find it on your hard drive (make sure it is still zipped) and upload it using the above interface. Once it is uploaded it will show up on your Manage Themes page here:

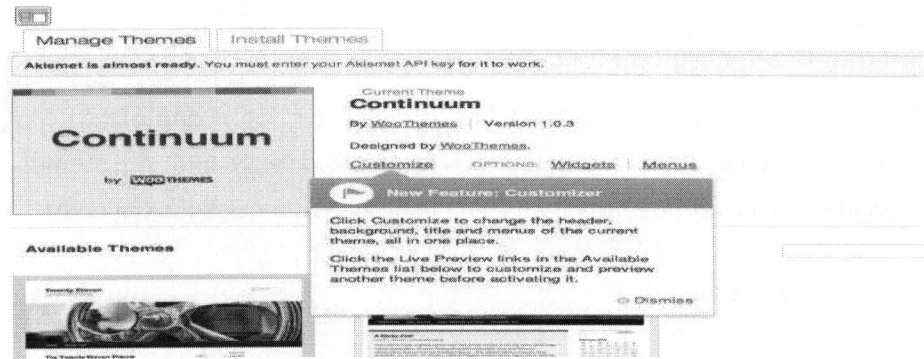

FTP Upload

If you decide to upload your theme via FTP instead, either because you cannot get the backend uploader to work or because you don't have it in a zip folder any longer, here is how to do it:

1. Unzip the folder.

2. Find the actual theme file. If you cannot find it, read the ReadMe file that likely appeared in the root after you unzipped.

3. Upload the theme folder to wp-content/themes/ on your server.

58

4. Go to Manage Themes under the Appearance menu and activate your theme.

It's as easy as that.

Plugins

Themes are basically the template for your website. They create an outline for everything you will upload to the site and make it possible to customize how content looks on every page.

Plugins, however, add new functionality to the site, sometimes to the way content looks and sometimes with actual new functions integrated directly into the site's layout. Themes can do an awful lot, but plugins have limitless potential. Here are some examples of cool things a plugin can do:

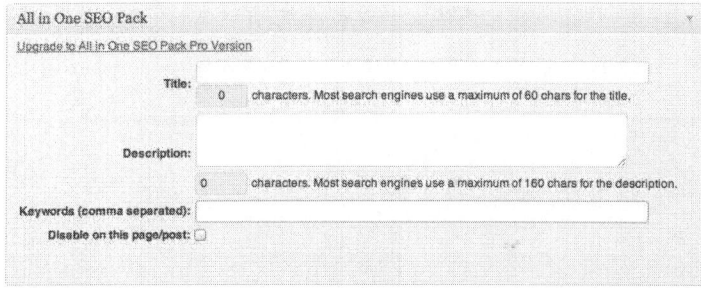

All-in-one SEO Pack

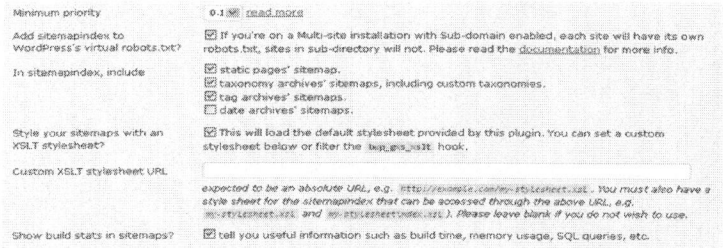

plugin and an old (or new) version of WordPress. Plugins need to be updated just like themes too, so if you use an old one that hasn't been updated in a few months or years, it probably won't work properly.

These are issues that can hamstring your website and give you a massive headache, so it's best to stick with handful of core, tested plugins. There are others, including some commercial plugins that add powerful functionality to your site, but the core ones will likely always work because of their popularity.

Core Plugins for Your WordPress Blog

Here are 10 of my favorite WordPress plugins – some very essential and others a little bit of fun:

1	All in One SEO
2	Google XML Sitemap Generator
3	W3 Total Cache
4	OIO Publisher
5	FD Feedburner Plugin
6	AskApache Password Protect
7	Login Lockdown
8	Show Top Commenters
9	MaxBlogPress Strip Ads
10	MaxBlogPress Ninja Affiliate

Most are free, some cost money, and all ten are on my site in some iteration, because I feel they offer significant value to my blog readers.

Graphics

Wordpress is incredibly flexible, so when you look at any theme, imagine being able to change quite literally anything you see with customized graphics, layouts or theme files. It's that simple. Of course, you don't necessarily need to spend a big pile of cash to make your site look amazing either. Look at my site for example:

I have a simple logo across the top and a few custom graphics such as the book for my list opt-in and my social media logos, but for the most part, I've kept it very simple.

Remember that this is a blog and the content on your blog is designed to do the talking. So, unless you are a designer or your audience expects a certain amount of flair, your site can look pretty straightforward and still be very effective.

At the same time, there are limits to just how straightforward it can look before it looks amateurish. Here's what I mean:

That's an ugly blog and it doesn't work for a number of reasons. Cheap looking banner, AdSense all over the place and content that doesn't flow from one section to the next. There are subtle differences so if you're having trouble finding the right balance, consider either a premium theme or hiring a designer who can help you tweak all of it.

Chapter Three:
Brand-o-Nomics

Building a blog based on Wordpress is easier now than it has ever been. It takes quite literally less than five minutes to create an entire website from scratch and get online. You probably surmised that much by how short the last chapter was. It's the definition of easy.

But that doesn't mean creating and running a blog is a breeze. Maintaining a blog is a lot of work, and while it is awesome to me that Wordpress has removed so much of the hard stuff from the technical side, it is also a little frustrating because it means that anyone can do it now and they don't always realize what they're getting into.

Luckily, you have an insider to help you navigate those choppy waters. That's what we're going to do next.

What I want to talk about now is your brand, your style, the tone and layout of your blog, and how all that can make it stand out from everyone else's. That's how you will really blow up your site and create a killer portal in your niche. Remember, just writing isn't enough. Just having ideas isn't enough. You need to present yourself in a way that is eye-catching and engaging to the people you communicate with. That's what a good brand does - it creates connections between people in ways that allow you access like you've never dreamed possible. And while there are a ton of tools to help you do this that I will go over later on, right now, as you're getting started, the focus needs to be on who you are and why anyone should care.

Who the Hell Are You?

My goal in this book is to teach you how to think from your readers' perspective. I want you to ask yourself what they want, what they see, what they think and how you can make it all better.

Should you always listen to them? Maybe not. But at least you will understand where they're coming from.

And one of the first questions anyone who lands on your site is going to ask, especially at first, is, "who the hell is this person?"

Imagine if you landed on a blog for the first time - a blog written by someone you didn't know. There are a few ways that blogger could capture your attention - a killer post that you bookmark, a funny tone that you appreciate or useful free stuff that you need. But regardless of all that, you need to know who this writer is and why you should trust their opinion on whatever it is they're writing about.

So, as a blogger, one of your first missions is to create a persona that permeates the entire blog. The writing style, the design, the topics you cover and the way you engage with comments - it all needs to be supported by a centralized and consistent persona that people can somehow relate to.

A lot of what we will discuss in throughout the book will address this very topic - how to present a unique and engaging personality that people can't help but love (or hate, but we'll get in that later).

When someone lands on JohnChow.com, I want them to think:

* The DotCom Lifestyle - I want someone to land on my site and see immediately that I am living the dream, but more importantly, I want them to know what that dream is (for me at least). Everyone interprets success differently, but I want to show my readers how it really looks - a guy who has the freedom to live life to its fullest and enjoy the things he has the opportunity to do.

* I'm a Simple Guy - I'm not a flashy guy. I don't go in for the fast cars and the exotic vacations or ostentatious lifestyle perks. I write a blog and when opportunities arise that I think will be fun I take advantage of them. That doesn't mean anything other than that I have made the most of my success - my blog reflects that.

* I Want to Help You - The goal of my blog is to help people. I'm not there to brag about what I've done (though I do often share my achievements and how I achieved them for illustrative purposes). What I want people to take away from my blog is that they can do the same and have fun doing it.

* You Can Reach Me Directly - I make it clear that I'm an open book. Leave a comment, contact me on Facebook or Twitter, join my mailing list - I will be in touch with you.

* It's All About the Content - The content takes centre stage on my site. When you land on my site there is a video from me to my readers and a handful of ads, but that's it. No big and flashy banners, no constant popups or voice narrations - just content that you can start reading immediately to learn more about what I do.

I want them to say "this guy is awesome, I'll come back and read more of his stuff later". I want them to think "Jim needs to read this" or "I'd better write a comment." I want a real response. The content being useful is not enough for me, nor will it be enough for most readers.

People are consumers. They spend all day finding and consuming information and entertainment. If the stuff you write, record, produce or draw isn't unique in some way, it might be useful to a reader, but that doesn't mean it will leave an impression. Will that reader say "Damn, this guy is awesome" or will it solicit more of a "cool..."?

So, when the time comes to answer the question, so to speak, of who the hell you are, consider a few of the following:

1. What do you believe about this niche?
2. How do you engage with people in real life?
3. Do you want to focus on news and announcements or "how to" pieces?
4. Do you have a comment strategy in place?
5. Do you encourage and facilitate integration of comments and conversation on your site?

More important than all of that, even, is what people think of you when they read something you write. Are they impressed? Annoyed? Encouraged? Enlightened? All four? It's a good question and one you should continue to ask *every single time* you write a blog post. The moment you stop asking yourself these questions is the moment your blog becomes just another website.

Seven Habits of Successful Bloggers

I wrote a post a few years ago and included it in my first eBook (now available for free on JohnChow.com) discussing the seven habits of highly successful bloggers.

I've reprinted them below for your reference, but I also want to go one step further.

This is stuff that will be touched upon throughout the book, but it can give you a good idea right now of how to position yourself as a powerful brand in your niche. Here are my seven habits along with some specific tips and recommendations for maintaining those habits:

1 – They Blog on a Consistent Basis

Successful bloggers are not on again off again bloggers. They pick a posting frequency and they stick to it no matter what. If you're going to do a new blog post every day, then make sure you do a new blog post every day. If you don't think you can handle that level of posting, then pick a number that you're more comfortable with.

It is better to post once per week and do it consistently than to start out posting once per day and then begin skipping days (or weeks). If you're new to blogging, I recommend you start with one to three posts per week and work up to a level that's comfortable for you. You should always increase the post frequency and never decrease it. If you do have to decrease for some reason, then do it very slowly.

2 – They Are Passionate about Their Topic

If you're not passionate about the topic you're blogging about, then you're going to have a really hard time growing the blog. Blogs attract like-minded people, and they will see right through you if you're just in it for the money. Being passionate about what your topic makes it easier to keep up with the industry – you want to find out what is happening in your niche because it's your passion and not just because it may make you money. I started this blog with no intention of making money from it. For the first eight months of the blog's life, it made zero and its traffic was just a few hundred readers per day. Yet, I updated the blog an average of over two posts per day during that period. You cannot do that unless you are passionate about your topic.

3 – They Interact with Their Readers

A blog is not a one-way street. In addition to providing information, a blog is a tool to facilitate communication between the blogger and his or her readers. Successful bloggers interact with their readers. They answer reader emails and comments, and they ask for feedback.

Interacting with your readers builds trust and loyalty, and it makes you more approachable. My biggest fear is that some readers would place me so high on a pedestal that they are scared to approach me. By keeping my blog on a light note and having fun with my postings, I feel I connect with my readers on a more personal level.

4 – They Give Out Lots of Link Love

Successful bloggers don't hoard their links. They don't have a problem with linking to a PR0 blog. They put the concerns of their readers ahead of a Google ranking. If another blog has a good story or idea on the topics I cover, I don't care what their PageRank is - I'm going to link to them.

Too many bloggers get caught up worrying about SEO and link count. They only want high ranking blogs linking to them and won't link to low ranking blogs. I've linked to hundreds of brand new zero ranked blogs and who knows how many zero ranked blogs have linked to me. This blog has a PageRank 6.

69

Some SEO guy told me if I would have been more careful about linking, I could have gotten a PageRank 7. My answer to that is, "People first, Google second."

5 – They Know How to Brand Themselves

Successful bloggers know how to brand. Branding will separate your blog from the millions of other ones out there. The most unique thing about your blog is not the topic you're writing about. What makes your blog stand out? The answer is simple – you! Your ability to promote and brand yourself will separate your blog from the pack.

Very few blogs have ever gotten big without some kind of tier-one level press coverage. This doesn't mean you need to hit the front page of the New York Times. You can turn any coverage into brand-building material. I'll have more on this in a future post.

Branding is one of the reasons I tell all bloggers to get their own domain name instead of going with a free service like Blogspot. You want to brand yourself, not them. Can you imagine Guy Kawasaki with a URL of GuyKawasaki.blogspot.com?

6 – They Are Good Writers

You do not have to be a great writer to have a successful blog but you do need to be good at getting your ideas across in an understandable manner. Most readers read blogs for information. They will forgive occasional grammar mistakes as long you can get your point across. If your readers are having troubling understanding what you're trying to say then you need to improve your writing skills.

7 – They Read John Chow dot Com

This is 100% true! Successful bloggers read other successful blogger's blogs. I check out all the big name bloggers every day to see what they are talking about. You are never too big to stop learning.

When to Post and How Long

As I stated above, how often you post is not as important as your consistency in posting. If you fail to post consistently, you will lose your audience no matter how good your content is. I have fallen into this trap more than a handful of times, but not once since I started having success in this field.

In fact, as I am writing this, I have more than one month's worth of blog posts prepared and scheduled for publication. I always aim to have at least one week's worth of posts ready and usually I am a bit ahead of that number, just to ensure I never miss a scheduled post. People expect to see a blog post from me every day, so if I don't post, they wonder what's wrong. More importantly, they use the time they would normally use to read my post to read someone else's. That's not good.

It only takes a few days like that to start shedding readers like a Pomeranian in Arizona. You have to be consistent - your readers will reward you for rewarding them.

So, what days should you post? It doesn't really matter as long as you post consistently. What time of day? This will depend largely on your niche and location, but it does matter. It is one of the key elements that I feel is not tested enough when it comes to posting. While I tend to feel that timing has a bigger impact on social media posting, it matters as much for blog posts in many cases (especially if you bolster your readership with social media a lot of the time).

I recommend starting with one of the two "prime time" posting hours - between 11am and 12pm and between 3pm and 5pm. These are the biggest "wasted hours" of the day - when workers spend more time on Facebook and Twitter than on their jobs. It's a great way to drive traffic through natural procrastination.

Remember, though, that the timing should relate to your audience not where you are. If you live in Croatia, but 90% of your audience is in the American midwest, aim to post your new content when *those people* are most likely to read it.

Length

A good question and one that will largely depend on your audience and the type of content they enjoy most. Some blogs thrive on long, detailed how-to articles between 1,000 and 3,000 words. Others get six figure reader counts with 250 and 300 word blog posts and others still use almost no text at all and focus heavily on video (mine is a combination of all three).

You'll find that the most effective way to build an audience is to provide a little bit of everything. Don't be afraid to write a really short blog post if you don't have much to say about a particular topic. At the same time, you should occasionally sit down and write something truly epic, filled with useful tips that your readers will eat up. They will appreciate it, I can guarantee you. And when you feel comfortable doing it, you should spend a few minutes recording videos - even if it's just you spitballing a little bit about what you think on a topic - the less formal the better in many cases.

As your blog grows and ages, you will start to learn more about your audience, both from the comments you receive and the data you find in Google Analytics. Using that data, you can start adjusting your content calendar to reflect what people actually want to read or watch. Don't assume you know what people want until you give them a little bit of everything and see how they respond.

Commenting within the Community

There are a number of different ways to build a following in the blogosphere, but few are as effective as going out there and showing what you know. Specifically, you should actively engage people in conversation.

I like to think of it this way. Imagine you walk into a room filled with perfect strangers intent on telling a story you think is hilarious. You know for a fact that people will find it funny, but you don't know anyone and don't want to interrupt everyone to tell it.

So, instead of pulling out a bullhorn and announcing your story to the room, you introduce yourself to people, ask them their names, listen to their stories and build some rapport.

You network.

And networking is exactly what a blog needs to thrive in a world filled with millions of other blogs.

Of course, you can't hop on a plane and visit every blogger and blog reader in your niche personally, so instead you post a comment on posts from other bloggers. This is the single most effective way to generate return traffic to your blog, build your reputation and ensure people are interested in what you have to say.

In chapters 7 and 8 I go into much greater detail on how to do this and provide some tips I've cultivated over the years to ensure you find the right blogs and engage with them in a way that will drive traffic to your site.

For now, just make it part of your daily routine. Pick out 10 or 20 blogs in your niche (go to Technorati or Google Blog Search and make a list) and start commenting on between 3 and 4 post per day. That's all it will take.

Monitoring the Blogosphere

How do you know where to comment, what people are
reading and what topics are hot in your niche at any given point in time? You cheat a little.

Listen, no one is everywhere at the same time. The bloggers that somehow manage to break story after story aren't super geniuses and don't run elaborate spy networks - they just happen to be very efficient at gathering and sifting through huge volumes of data very quickly.

Here are my secret tools and how I use them to ensure I know exactly what people are talking about and what they want me to talk about.

1. **Google Alerts** - Google Alerts allows you to define specific search terms and then track whenever a new page matching that term enters Google's index. If it's your name or company name, every one of your posts should create an alert. But so too will alerts be created for topics or keywords you define.

2. **Analytics** - Analytics is a free Google service that will show you to see where traffic comes from to your site and how people interact with your site in real time.

3. **RSS Readers** - I follow big blogs in my niche and have them delivered to my desktop via an RSS reader. This means that whenever a competitor or complementary blog topic enters the index I get a message telling me about it via the RSS reader.

4. **App Sales** - Check Google Play, Amazon or the iTunes App Store to see which pieces of software are hitting it big (usually outside of games and photo, unless those are your niches).

5. **Amazon Trends** - Amazon posts trending data for the products and categories on its site as well so you can see what is selling and where it is selling in real time. You can even see the percentage of change that occurs on the site.

6. **Google Trends** - Check Google Trends to see what keywords are trending each day and what news stories are being written about those topics.

7. **Twitter Search (TweetHub)** - You can search on Twitter to see what is tracking with higher numbers of tweets per hour, day or week. There are monitoring services as well that allow you to search through Tweets for mentions of your brand or blog.

8. **Facebook Search Insights** - Facebook has a less powerful search tool (unless you have a Page), but it can still be used in conjunction with third party apps to see what is being searched for most at any given time.

9. **Huffington Post** - The Huffington Post basically goes out and gathers content from top sites and consolidates them into a single news source. It's called curation and they've been doing it for a while, meaning you can find content on any topic here, and usually it will be among the most relevant sources for each niche.

This is a diverse list and I don't necessarily check everything every single day, but by having all of them at hand, I can make rapid decisions about how to respond to hot new topics.

Create your own list of secret research tools (or borrow mine!)

Claim Your Territory

Listen, the web is the world's premier space for sharing, but it's also a land grab. If you don't act fast, you'll be shit out of luck. So, you need to act fast, BEFORE you become well known, because that's exactly when people will start snapping up your name. Here's what I mean.

Direct Name Matches

A lot of very famous people (and some not so famous people) have been very successful in managing multiple accounts with different names on them, or in using a branded name instead of their actual name. But, would you prefer to market yourself as "dogtrainingdude535" or as "AmandaStein" on Twitter or Facebook. Which is easier and which is more natural?

Some of you won't be so lucky. It's almost 2013 and that means there are a lot fewer domain names and social properties available than 8 years ago when I got started, but a lot of you will still do quite well with this. Here are some tips to ensure you get as close to a direct name match for your accounts as possible.

1. **DotCom Matters, but Less with Name Match** - If you can get YOURNAME.net or YOURNAME.org, don't fret about the DotCom issue. Yes, a dotcom is better because it is more recognizable to potential readers, but if

you have a direct name match, it won't matter in terms of SEO and it's better for branding if you can match your name.

2. **Use KnowEm.com Liberally** - KnowEm.com is a tool you can use to instantly see where your name is available on sites like Facebook, Twitter, Blogger, etc. There are more than 200 social networks and another couple hundred bookmarking networks and other sites that you can check for name availability. Pay them a few extra bucks and they will register them for you too, but that's not necessary.

3. **Snag EVERYTHING** - If you find your name available, take a few hours one day and get all of them. You may not use anything but your blog and a couple social networks, but if some random service someday explodes in popularity you want to know you can have your name on that site.

4. **Don't Get Cute Unless You Have No Choice** - Avoid cute names or hyper-branded names that don't actually make sense. It might be cool and it might be fun to play with, but it's a lot harder to brand something like "Autaclanda" than "AmandaStein.com".

5. **Focus on the Big Three and Get One That Matches** - You want your core accounts and sites to match as much as possible. So start with your domain name and try to find one that is available both on Twitter and Facebook. This will keep the length of your domain name down too. Twitter handles can only be up to 15 characters, so keep it at that or lower if possible.

I'm talking a lot about direct name matches like JohnChow.com, but remember that this applies for any brand, including the name of a company you own or a book you've written. Claim your territory now so you can control it in the future.

More on Branding

The depth of your brand will depend on a lot of things. For example, on JohnChow.com, the brand is me. I don't need a fancy site because I have my name and face on it and a lot of people associate me with success in blogging - voila, I have a blog about successful blogging. It works well.

But, if you are running a blog about another topic (which many of you will do), there are a few other things to keep in mind. The brand will be new and different, and it will have a unique identity apart from you.

So there has to be an overarching theme, and that means you need to define your message.

Let's look at how to do this.

1. What Is the Message?

I know you're not a born marketer, or if you are, you probably aren't reading this chapter too carefully because, heck you probably have a lot of ideas you want to get into play.

So for those of you without the innate selling skills of Don Draper, consider for a moment what you should be doing with your brand. In other words, what do you want people to say when they describe your blog?

If someone were to ask one of your loyal readers, "what type of blog is it?" how would they answer?

It doesn't matter really what that answer is - it just matters that it matches your vision of the site, because you have enough control to ensure that's what happens. You can determine if the blog is seen as an authority on a given topic, for example, by writing long, authoritative posts. Or you can be funny, or cynical, or just silly. It doesn't matter what you decide, but it does matter that you take the time to define it and that you stick with that definition as you build out your site.

2. Disseminating Your Message

Once you know what you want to say, it's time to say it. Stop planning and start acting. The planning stages of any large project can be overwhelming because you end up spending more time trying to figure out what your site will look like than actually building that site.

So, stop thinking and start doing.

More importantly, make sure you are clear in your message when you write a post. Write content that reflects well on you and your site, or at least content that honestly represents what you think. Don't take advantage of linking opportunities or sell your blog space to a cause so you can make a quick buck.

Readers can sniff out a sellout quick and you don't want to be the funny smell they find when they do.

3. Staying On Message

It's easy to stay on message if you truly believe that message. The most important thing here is to avoid becoming too reactionary. As your brand grows and people start to trust your opinion and look to you for information about key topics and happenings in your niche, it's important that you don't suddenly change course on something you've previously said.

You'll be called out on it, and your reputation will suffer as a result.

Of course, it's easy to keep your message consistent if you simply avoid changing your opinion to fit someone else's or to make a quick buck.

4. Spreading Your Message

Use every tool at your disposal to get your opinion out there. Your brand becomes more ubiquitous and easier to trust when your readers see it literally everywhere. The key thing here is to create supplemental content. Create things that match up with each other - blog posts that fit with your Facebook posts that fit with your Tweets that reference your videos.

Don't just post the same content on every channel - use each channel's unique features to create content that fits your audience.

The Last Word on Branding

Some people don't like the "B" word because it makes a blog sound too corporate. I don't mind it, probably because I started as a marketer, but also because it is accurate. A blog is a brand as sure as Coke is a brand.

If you want your site to be successful, you need to determine in advance how you want people to see it when they visit.

Of course, that vision can change over time - as much as you need it to. If you find that the vast majority of people visiting your site want to see videos of you being sarcastic about a topic, then that might become your brand. Just be careful - don't let your message be co-opted by a vocal minority and try to avoid moving away from what you enjoy and are passionate about.

One of the only real ways to build a truly successful blog is to ensure that you enjoy what you are doing with it.

Chapter Four:
Content is Duke, Prince, King, Supreme Overlord - You Name It

I find the ruckus the last few years over Google Panda to be more than a little amusing. While Google has certainly dinged a handful of people who didn't deserve it, the vast majority of people who lost ranking had it coming. Let's face it, those sites weren't very good.

The goal of a website, remember, is not to make money. It's not to rank in Google or to have more pages than another site. It is to provide something of value to a visitor. So, when you create a website that is filled with content effectively replicated from another site, the results are going to be less than stellar.

Content truly is king and Google has finally upgraded their algorithm enough that we get to do more than just say it; we get to live it.

A website that doesn't focus first and foremost on creating interesting, valuable content is one that will not do well in search. I don't care if you have a mind-blowing concept and thousands of backlinks - if your site is just one page of bland content, you're going to miss out on a lot of possible traffic.

This is a blog, my friend, and a blog is built around content. From top to bottom, your site is a temple to content in whatever niche you decide to write about. So you need to find ways to write original, interesting, engaging content that is unique from other content in your niche.

Don't just ask what people would want to read (and subsequently write a blog based on what other people have written before you) - ask what kinds of content you can create that will blow people away unexpectedly. That's how you create content that will be shared and reshared dozens or hundreds of times.

I didn't know this post was going to blow up, but sure enough I got tens of thousands of hits in a matter of hours. I still get hits on that page. It's mind blowing.

You need to find your "Trading Hours for Dollars" moment - something that will blow away your readers and capture the imagination of other bloggers and social media users in ways you never could have expected.

Let's create some killer content.

First, Be Awesome

What exactly is "awesome"?

It depends. Who is reading your content? What kinds of things do they tend to enjoy? Will they share it? Comment on it? Ask questions about it? Write about it on their own site?

In most cases, the path to awesomeness is the shortest one available. Yeah, you need to do research, and yes, you need to spend a fair amount of time testing the waters of your niche. But really, to be awesome you just need to have fun with what you're doing.

Am I awesome?

Of course.

And it's because I love what I write about. Even this far in and with so many engagements behind and ahead of me, I love running a blog and I love interacting with the people who read the content on that blog. I get a little rush every time I see a new comment pop up, even when it's a scathing criticism (and I do get plenty of those).

I see opportunities at every turn, and when other people would get discouraged or overwhelmed, I feel inspired.

It's a weird business model, but it gives me a type of freedom you would never believe - allowing me to write about things and do things that I could never have done in another job. I'm an artist and a journalist and I take that role very seriously.

You should too.

I can't define "awesome" for you - all I can say is, don't try too hard. Don't go out and try and emulate other blogs or write content that fits a certain mold.

Don't look at my blog and say "how can I rewrite that post to be in my own voice?" Find your own voice. Be your own content editor - be your own producer. Enjoy what you write and your readers will enjoy it too.

And ultimately, you will be awesome.
Of course, there are a few shortcuts you can take too, which is what I want to show you next.

Viral Content at a Glance

The whole idea of viral content is that it can take on a life of its own. Here's an example:

When I was blogging about the ways I was making money online, people ate up those posts. Whenever I posted a new earnings report, it would get shared over and over again, immediately going viral, because people ate up that content. I recognized what people wanted and put it on my blog.

Those posts were written, posted on a blog and then left to their own devices. Because they fulfilled the needs of my audience, they spread rapidly and effectively went "viral", drawing a large volume of traffic to the site very rapidly.

There are a few ways to define viral content. I could try and dissect it for you and explain how it should look or what it will do when released into the wild, but probably the best way to explain it is to provide some examples and talk about why each of them was effective.

In every one of these cases, the content created was not somehow "better" than any other post, image or video. It was simply more timely, more engaging, more tuned to the sensibilities of its readership.

For me, viral content needs to be one or more of the following:

1   **Authoritative** – It's not good enough to be informative. A post that is going to take on a life of its own needs to be peerless. There should be no other blog post or video out there that can compete with what you're creating.

2   **Entertaining** – If you want to see entertaining content in action, check out YouTube. Bloggers and video creators alike generate tens of thousands of entertaining videos a day that go viral just because they are fun to watch.

3   **Hilarious** – Funny stuff is by far the easiest to get to go viral. Of course, being funny is not easy. But look at what Ben Huh was able to do with LOLCats. Simple, quick to create images and posts that get HUGE traffic because every single one of them gets shared rapidly.

4   **Jaw-Dropping** – If you can, create something that will blow the minds of your target audience. A blog post that eviscerates a point of view or an image that is just too good not to share will become a viral piece of content. What is jaw-dropping? It depends on your niche and your audience, but you'll often know it when you see it.

5   **Controversial** – This is the form of viral content I like the least. Controversy drives some serious traffic, and people will share what you wrote simply so they can point and say "do you believe this?" But before you write something in this vein, make sure you actually want that kind of attention. Controversy sells for sure, but it also brands you in a certain way that you may not necessarily like and that can be harder to control.

That's it folks.

Viral content is immensely powerful. It can draw attention from tens of thousands, even millions of eyeballs if you do it right – but there is no formula to get it done. You'll get a feel for it over time and may even get good at it one day as you come to understand your audience, but there will never be a cookie cutter formula for it.

And to be perfectly honest, there doesn't have to be.

Most blogs don't have a lot of break-out posts. That's why they're called break-out posts. They only happen once in a very great while. Instead, you'll find most blogs grow at a steady rate, adding new readers on a weekly or even monthly basis and growing carefully as you provide regular, reliable content.

If one of those posts breaks out and draws mega traffic, awesome – if not, well you're still growing. Heck, eventually people might share everything you write just for the hell of it.

You can be awesome without going viral and you can go viral without being awesome – your goal is to be consistent and hopefully you'll be both.

Forget the Search Engines

Later in the book I'm going to talk about some SEO strategies I have used to great success for my blog. None of them involve keyword stuffing, on-site optimization or overhauls.

A blog is naturally search engine friendly. It has lots of keywords in each URL, it has a complex yet highly organized linking structure, it has plugins that send out loads of tags and categories for indexing – everything the search engines could ever want structurally is right there.

What they don't have right off the bat is content.

87

If you build a blog for search engines, it's much more likely that the only readers you'll have are search engines. Your blog is for people, lots and lots of people. And with time, the search engines will see all those people returning to your blog and you'll get credit for it, but the buck doesn't start or stop there. It's content that matters.

I like to think of myself as a content entrepreneur.

I've built a hell of a business out of my blog, but I don't create a product or sell a service. I write blog posts and record videos. I make the occasional appearance on radio or TV. I'm selling my opinion on things that matter to people and it works.

The search engines give me credit for that effort, but only because I've worked so hard to create a persona trusted first by people, then by machines.

You must do the same. Create a content plan that focuses on what you can offer of value to your readers, NOT to the search engines, and it will have a much bigger long-term impact.

Plus, when Google releases its next animal-themed algorithm update, you'll be ready for whatever changes they make.

The Content Kaleidoscope

When I say "content" most people think I'm talking about text content - the blog posts I write on a daily basis.

Most of the time I am, but to be perfectly honest with you, written content is only one small part of the much larger picture. To be successful as a blogger, you need to widen your vision and take advantage of the full palette of options available to you.

How much of the home page is devoted to actual 500 word blog posts?

About a third.

This is not an anomaly. This is one of the biggest blogs on the Internet, and the owner, Darren Rowse, has created a formula that works incredibly well for his audience. More importantly, it works for the types of technology and communications tools we are currently using to communicate with that audience.

Here's how I think of content choices. Every person out there who might read my blog has a different learning style. They like to absorb information in different ways, and so I strive to create content that fits as many of those ways as possible.

For those that like in-depth commentary, I write lots of carefully manicured blog posts. For readers that like to skim information and pull out only what matters most to them, I fill my blog posts with bulleted lists and lots of H2 headings to make it scannable. For those that like visual representations, I ensure there is at least one image for every 500 words of text. And for videophiles, I post a handful of videos every month covering more in-depth topics.

A blog is not a newspaper column - it is a web column. And a web column needs to be as versatile and interactive as the web. Which is why content is a broad term that can describe any of the following:

Videos

For whatever reason, when I talk to people about the types of content they can include on their blog, the vast majority of them see video as being one of the most complicated, but for me it is the simplest.
Consider for a moment what a video consists of. There is a bit of upfront investment as you have to purchase the equipment needed to record. But after that, it takes as little as 10 minutes to sit down in front of a camera and discuss a few things with your readership.

While there are certainly ways to create more inventive, content-rich videos, the cool part is that you don't really need to. Video succeeds not because it is big and complicated but because it is simple and straightforward. There is less artifice, less sleight of hand. If you are genuine with your audience, your videos will personalize you and your brand in ways that written content rarely can.

Furthermore, there are very few good excuses *not* to use video for your blog. If you own a laptop, it almost certainly has a webcam, and even if it doesn't, you can buy a USB plug-and-play webcam for less than $30. The software to record is free and the storage for those videos is also free (YouTube, Vimeo, Facebook, etc.) So, the only real thing that still stands in the way of most people who want to create videos is their own discomfort in doing so, and honestly that's not a very good excuse. Unless you have crippling stage fright, you will gain far more than you lose by creating videos for your blog.

Creating Killer Video Content

Would that I could leave you just with that, but the truth is that, because it is so easy to create video these days, you can't *quite* get away with recording anything and expecting a boost in traffic because of it. You need to create something interesting and engaging, and whatever the content is designed to do, it should be injected with your personality - something that a lot of videos lack (for a variety of reasons).

If you look at my blog, you'll see videos on almost every post - especially anything related to me personally. Longer, written posts are often sans video as they cover a how-to topic or show people a list of useful tools in my field, but when I cover an event I attended or a new product, I almost always include video.

Why?
Because, it makes sense. If my personality is on display in a post, I create a video to ensure it is really on display - that people can see me sharing my opinion or experiences related to that product or topic. And it works quite well.

When someone lands on my website, the first thing they see is a video of me introducing them to the site. When they click on a review, I often greet them and show them my experiences. When they click on a news report about an event I attended, they often see me patrolling the floor of that event.
You can make video about nearly anything, but the stuff that really takes off is the stuff that only you can make - the personally derived content that shows your opinion, your experiences and your lifestyle. Of course, the more interesting you can make it, the better it will perform.

Podcasts

Podcasts are big. Whether because everyone now has a phone with Internet capability and podcasts are ridiculously small in file size (comparatively), podcasts have become exceptionally popular among a wide range of demographics. More importantly, they give you a third avenue to spread content to your readers, and subsequently, a lot more websites on which to post that content.

But how do you create a podcast that matches the content on your blog while offering a lot more to your readers/listeners?

Here are a few tips to getting a podcast put together that matches what you want your site to achieve:

1. **Choose a Specific Topic** - More even than a blog, your podcast needs to be as specific as possible. That's not to say you should record only about one type of product in your niche, but you shouldn't try to cover everything either. I like to carve out topics that are unique to me and my niche, and it works extra well for a podcast. Take Kevin Smith's "Fat Man on Batman" podcast for example. He could have made a podcast about comic books or movies, but no, he got as specific as possible and created one about Batman. And it was in the top 25 for three months. What are you passionate about? What could you sit and talk about for hours? That's your podcast topic.

2. **Build a Cast** - A good podcast is rarely just one person. If you're the only person on your podcast, find people to interview. If you don't have the street cred to land a big interview yet, get a cohost. Find a way to create some type of synergy in your production. People like to hear people talking about things - it sounds more natural. Otherwise, you're doing an audio book. A podcast is

92

like a radio show and a radio show is almost never just one person (unless you take call ins or something similar).

3. **Make a List of Content Ideas** - Sit down and write out as many content ideas as possible. A big, huge list is best because it gives you something to come back to in the future whenever you are running low on ideas. A podcast will be slightly more produced than a blog post because it is longer. You need to be able to talk for at least 25 minutes and upwards of an hour, and while people like those fly on the wall type podcasts where you just babble for a while about something interesting, you still need a semblance of a script to ensure you're staying on topic.

4. **Get the Equipment** - The free webcam and microphone on your laptop may cut mustard for a Skype call, but they are not going to work to record a podcast. At the very least, get a headset with microphone and noise cancellation (usually less than $50) so you can get your voice and nothing else. If you have the money and are dedicated to the idea of a podcast, a microphone like the Blue Yeti or anything from Rode is equally good.

5. **Practice, Practice, Practice** - Don't assume that you'll put together an award-winning, iTunes-topping podcast the first time out. Probably you'll stink. These things are hard. You wouldn't think that talking into a microphone with a friend or two for 45 minutes would be that difficult, but it is, and it can be draining. So the first few podcasts are learning experiences. Distribute them early and market them normally, but don't expect much out of them - this is how you get better.

6. **Record and Distribute** - Finally, get that podcast out to the public. There are a few dozen sites that distribute these things - including SoundForge. Keep in mind that iTunes does NOT distribute podcasts. It is more like an

93

RSS feed for podcasts. So, you need to upload it somewhere else and then post the URL for it to iTunes. You can also distribute that URL through Facebook and Twitter and on your own blog. Another great way to ramp up interest is to record a video of your podcast and put it both on iTunes and video sharing sites like YouTube and Vimeo.

There are long, in-depth books available about how to create and distribute a podcast, but to keep it as simple as possible, a good podcast is the equivalent of an audio blog. It is designed to provide value to your listeners, it must be done regularly so they can expect it and it builds on its previous successes, reaching out to people on social media and creating an audience that will spread it to new people when you create interesting, high quality content.

Photos

You can do a lot with photos. You can create a post entirely devoted to images, or you can use them to supplement your existing posts. You can even go the LolCats route and simply add a caption to a funny photo and set it loose on the public. All of these are effective uses of photos, but whatever you do, it's important that you have a clear idea of what role photos will play on your site.

Here's what I recommend.

Every single post you put up should have an image in it - at least one image for every 500-600 words of text you write. So if you slap together a 2,000 word post, you should have 4 images in that post.

In each image you should include the following:

94

* **Alt Tags** - The alt tag tells the browser what text to display whenever the mouse appears over that image. It's important not only for user experience but to tell the search engine what your image is of.

* **Caption** - Captions can be funny or informative but they should be useful for your readers, not just filler. They also have a great positive impact on search rankings.

* **SEO Friendly File Name** - Rename any files from the big long string of numbers and letters to an SEO friendly file name.

Why all the work? Because it will ensure your photo gets indexed in Google image search which can increase traffic by as much as 60% in some cases (people REALLY like to search for images).

Now, what about actually creating posts around images?

I personally don't do this. For my audience an image (unless it's an infographic) is not very useful. So, I don't post images unless they are very useful. If I want to post just an image because I think it is cool or funny, I do that on Facebook or Twitter where it better fits the audience.

Lists

One of the most common forms a blog post can take (and also one of the most popular) is the list. A list post relays a large volume of information in an easy to read format while creating a great backlinking opportunity at the same time. It also gives you the option to write other posts that extrapolate on that list in the future, or you can simply feature that list as a core part of your site. So how do you create a good list for your blog?

First, ask what types of things would be of most value to your readers.If you run a blog about Wordpress plugins, a list of the best themes for Joomla might be relevant, but much less so than a list of Wordpress themes. At the same time, there are dozens of different options for things that would work. Here are some examples:

* Free Resources - Most niches have a lot of great resources online. You can do your readers a service by gathering those resources into a single, easy to reference list. People will gladly reference it on their own sites and you'll probably get a few link backs from those sites.

* Cool Things - If you think something is cool, why not put together a big list of ALL the things you think are cool in your niche? From funny videos to really amazing books you've read, there are a lot of ways to fill a list like this.

* Tips - Write up a list of tips on a specific topic in your niche. Here's an example from my site: http://www.johnchow.com/five-things-to-do-when-you-have-nothing-to-blog-about/. It's not a catch-all for tips in my industry, but a specific sub-niche that I have created a list of tips for.

* Secrets - Are there secret strategies, tips or other hidden details in your niche that you feel you have access to and other people do not? Then create a list and put it on your site. You can be a mind blower or you can simply gather things that people know into a single, easy to access resource right at their fingertips.

* Other Bloggers - What about other bloggers? Are there are a lot of people you read and respect that you'd like to share with your readers. Not only is this a useful tactic, but it can get you in good with a lot of these bloggers when you start generating links to their sites.

*Specific Posts on Your Site - When you start putting together larger numbers of posts you can curate them yourself. Create lists of useful posts on your site and share them with people. I did that in my free eBook and again here.

The goal of a list is not just to create a list. Writing a 500 word post with the "top 3 reasons for x....." is fun, but not always useful to your readers. If you want your content to be truly useful to your readers, what you need to do is create a list that gathers divergent content that other people may not have access to into a single resource. That's when you'll really create something cool.

Infographics

Infographics are hot right now. They always have been, but right now they are one of the most effective ways to get guest post opportunities and guest post opportunities are one of the most effective ways to generate links to your site in a way that Google approves of. So, I want to talk a little about what makes a good infographic and what makes a bad one.

First, what does an infographic do?

People falsely assume that a good infographic is anything that shows information within a graphic format on a site. This is not true. An infographic is an image that informs readers through graphical representations of data. It's pop-data visualization, and because so few people understand what this even means, most of them get it dead wrong.

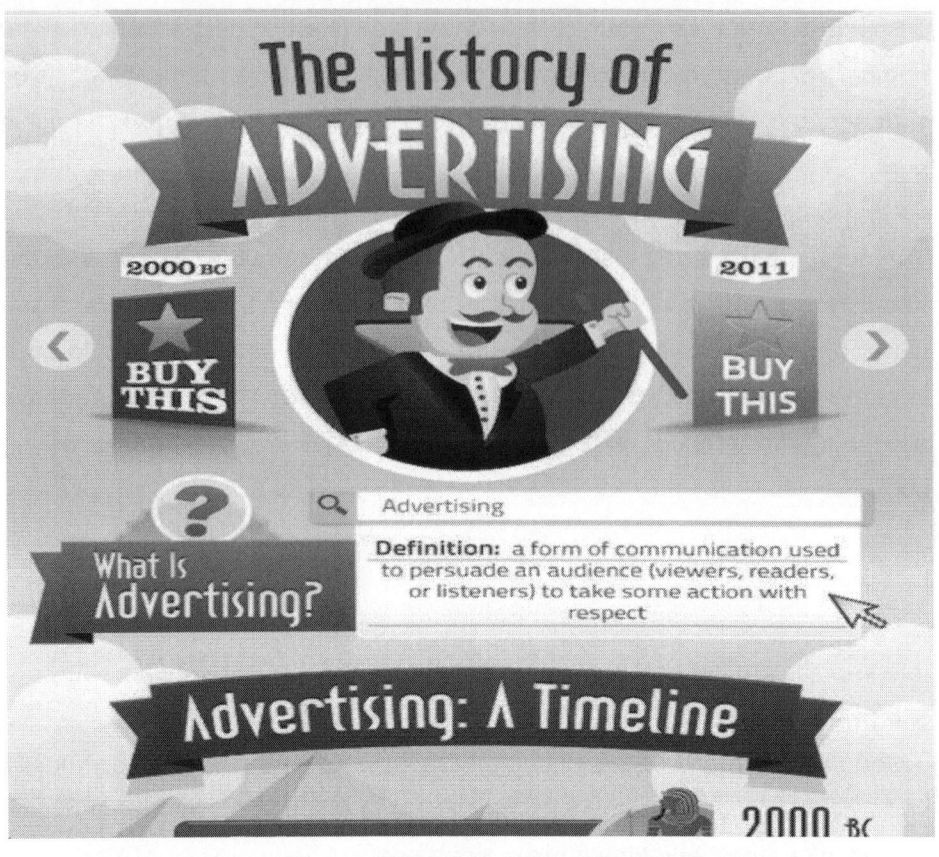

Here is an infographic I distributed on my site recently. I didn't create it of course - it was from Infolinks, where I know a few of the creators. But it had the same effect. It's a great infographic because it takes a topic of direct interest to my readers and displays it in a killer, fun-looking way.

How do you do the same?

Well, if you're a graphics guy, you can create one. But if you're not, the best you can do is hire someone or snag some software that will create one for you. I would recommend the former if you have the money for it, but I wouldn't recommend doing that until you have a large enough network in place to distribute that infographic rapidly and get some solid feedback on it.

A good infographic is important because it is often shared rapidly and people like to share that content. The difference is that you need to make sure it is also interesting - not just an infographic. Poorly done infographics won't get shared any faster or any more substantially than a poorly written blog post.

More Content Ideas

I saw this infographic on CopyBlogger a few days before writing this section and had to share it because it is loaded with good ideas about how to build your blog with great content:

http://www.copyblogger.com/create-content-infographic/

As a side note relating to our last section on infographics, what they did was to take a blog post by one of their writers: http://www.copyblogger.com/create-content-ideas/ and give it to the infographic team of BlueGlass, an infographic development specialist, and created the following. Here are a few of my favorites - ones that I use frequently for my own sites - from the infographic:

*Curation - This is popular right now but often done wrong, for a variety of reasons. To start, people think that "curation" is a fancy word for "plagiarize". Let's look at what this actually means. First, curation means that you go out and take select pieces of things and create a new whole out of it. For example, a museum exhibition is curated to look a certain way and give off a certain vibe. They don't just throw a bunch of old stuff in a room and say "have at". It's about what *isn't* there as much as what is. Additionally, curation in blog format requires that you include additional content to personalize it in

99

some way. You can't just reprint someone else's blog post and say you're curating content on that topic. You should take small pieces from that blog post, quote them and then write your response to them. A good curated post is one that includes multiple snippets from other blogs with interjections from you on the same topic.

Interview Someone - An interview is a quick and easy way to integrate new content without having to think of anything beyond the questions you will ask. This adds the personal experience of whoever you interview and lends new credibility to your blog for landing such an interview.

Case Studies - Case studies work in both directions - either the good or the bad on any given topic. I like them a lot because they offer me a chance to take everything I know and have been talking about and apply it to a situation outside my sphere of influence. For instance, I could write a post about what a company like Coca Cola is doing right with their social media marketing campaigns. That's a great way to build off of my blog and show that I know what I'm talking about. Or I could find a corporate blog that is only updated every 12-19 days and write about what they are doing wrong (and what they could do to fix the problem). Case studies, even if they are just observational, offer real world applications for what you are writing about and people love them.

Your Failures and Successes - You can take the case study concept one step further and make one out of yourself. What you have *you* done right or wrong in your career and what can people learn from it? You'd be surprised how much people will eat this kind of thing up. It's the same reason people love interviews so much. They want to know what you have been doing and what they can learn from it. It's an opportunity for them to take lessons from someone who is in the place they want to be or who knows things they want to know. Plus, it brings you back down to earth. You're showing how you live

100

the same kind of life as them and sometimes make the same (or worse) mistakes.

* Name Recognition Tips - This is my favorite from the Copyblogger list - mash up two completely unrelated topics to create a new post topic that just sounds interesting. Their example of batman and blogging is great but it can work with anything. They're easy to make up too and you can write practically anything to support the position you take. *What Bilbo Baggins Teaches Us About Traveling and Retirement. The Avengers Guide to Spring Cleaning.* Seriously, anything you can think of will work, and then you can have fund mixing and matching metaphors between the characters and the story you're trying to tell.

* Pop Culture - At the same time, you can write a blog post that uses pop culture in almost any way you see fit. There are a number of ways to do this. The above is great, but so too are reviews, anecdotes about "what you were doing when...", reminders about things in your niche, or things in your niche that actually relate to pop culture. Heck, you can even just watch TV shows and see if you can get any good ideas from them. What movies or music does your target audience like? Now watch and listen and get ideas.

* Stop Blogging and Start Consuming - If you are drawing a blank on ideas for your blog, take a break. Watch a movie. Go for a walk. Read a book. Do something unrelated, but keep the back of your mind open so you're constantly looking out for ideas of what you can say and do to generate new content ideas. There are millions of really great ideas out there floating around. Keep your mind open and you'll find them.

* Recycle Old Content - If all else fails, dig up some old content and recycle it. Do you have 100 posts on your blog? All of them could be redone as videos or integrated into podcasts or reshaped into infographics. Think of creative ways to build new and exciting content for your blog even if it just means taking stuff you already wrote and dumping it into the blender.

* Personal Stories - Personal stores are great, but only if you relate them to your site. Don't tell people about what you ate for breakfast unless it somehow has something to do with your niche. It doesn't take much effort to connect two seemingly unrelated things though. Try this exercise. Whenever you are blogging, ask yourself if anything has happened in your life that is similar or related to that topic. If so, put it in the post. Eventually, you'll start thinking in those terms automatically and your posts will benefit from it.

There Are More

This is just a short list of possible ways you can share information, ideas and beliefs you have with your target audience. Don't let it hold you back - be creative, be insightful and be willing to try new things whenever you have an idea that may not fit someone's mold. That's the cool thing about blogging - you can do practically anything you want and it will resonate with some segment of your audience.

Attracting Comments

One of the most frequent questions I get from readers and students alike is how to attract more comments. There's nothing more satisfying that seeing 10 or 20 people leave a comment about something you wrote or recorded.

Of course, at the same time, there is nothing more frustrating than writing a 1,500 word review or recording a 10 minute video and not getting a single piece of feedback from your audience. So I get a lot of people approaching me, often more than a little frustrated with their lack of success in this regard, asking how to get more comments.

Before I get into some of the ways that I drive commenting on my blog, let me dispel some myths about what comments mean and why some blogs tend to get less of them than others (and always will).

* People Don't Like to Comment - The vast majority of people don't like to comment. Forget thinking to do it (which most people don't) - you'll be hard pressed to find anyone that actually wants to comment on something they've read. They feel they need to have something good to say - something engaging or interesting. This is not the case, of course, and part of your job is to remind them of that.

* Participation Ranges Between 0.1 and 1% - Actual participation rates across the Internet tend to average between 1 in 100 and 1 in 1000 *active* readers. By "active" I mean someone who actually sits down and finishes an entire blog post, not just unique visitors to your blog according to Google Analytics. This number varies a lot and you can improve it quite a bit with some of the tips I'll show you soon. Obviously there is a big difference between 0.1% and 1%, but if you can get above that rate, you'll be doing quite well.

* Negativity Drives More Comments - One of the tough things about human nature that you'll need to overcome is that people are MUCH more willing to say something negative than something positive. It's why negative reviews can often outweigh positive reviews for a new product. It's why consumption-based services like Amazon.com or iTunes and the App Store actively prod their customers to leave reviews. People don't leave reviews (and in turn, comments) unless they're a little annoyed. But there is a catch. The same urge to participate and share a negative experience can be triggered by a positive experience if the experience is strong enough. Some say that it needs to be 10 times as strong a feeling - your job is to create content *that good*.

103

* Reciprocation is Vital in Commenting - If you want people to comment, you have to return the favor. Comment on other blogs, mention comments in your posts and reply to *every single comment* you receive because when you engage with people back, you drive repeat comments and it steam rolls from there.

* People Follow Others - A funny thing happens to most new blogs. When a blog is new and there are no comments on it, it's *extremely* hard to drive the first few comments. I've seen blogs getting upwards of 2,000 active readers a day that simply couldn't drive a comment. The funny thing is, though, that most of those blogs will surge in comments once one or two regular commenters starts leaving thoughts on posts. So find someone who wants to talk and talk back - you'll reap the rewards from growing such relationships.

The cards may seem stacked against you, but like anything related to blogging, if you over deliver, it won't matter. People respond to that kind of enthusiasm and will ultimately be much more willing to engage with what you have written as a result.

Handling Negative Comments

Let's face it, you're not always going to get positive reactions to your posts. Over time you will start to see more than a handful of people go off on you for any number of things. They may not like what you said, they may read what you said wrong, or they may simply decide they don't like you and want to get some attention.

This is the Internet and some people have issues that have little to do with you. It's not the negative comments you receive, but how you handle them when they come in.

104

Accept and Use Negative Comments

A lot of people think of negative comments as a bad thing. But when I get a negative comment, especially on a new blog, I am excited because the site is growing. A small percentage of readers will take the time to write something negative, so if your negative comment rate increases, it probably means that the readership for your site is increasing as well. Like I say, if you're not pissing someone off, you're not doing it right.

Of course, plenty of people read this the wrong way and think, "Let's go piss some people off to grow the blog". That's a bad course of action too. You shouldn't create a blog designed to annoy your readers. The goal should always be to delight and inform, but if you happen to step on a few toes in the process, so be it - there is nothing wrong with that. Never change what you are writing or how you write it to please the minority of people who happen to dislike it.

Discussions Grow Out of Negativity

It's hard to have a conversation if every comment you receive is "wow, that's amazing, thanks!" It might be heartening, but it doesn't build a community. Like them or not, negative comments serve an important purpose, generating camaraderie between you and your readers and helping you flesh out discussions more fully. This is not only good for the health of your blog (assuming you keep negative comments under control to avoid anything hurtful or hateful), but it can generate a lot more traffic for your blog which is always a good thing. I don't delete a lot of comments because I believe people have the right to say what they want and because I want to foster conversation about the stuff I publish. If someone goes too far, I will act, but only then.

Keep in mind too that while a lot of people threaten leaving the community on your site or boycotting your site because of something you said, they almost never do. Leaving would mean they don't care, and if they didn't care, I can guarantee they wouldn't take the time to leave a comment like that. They might continue to leave negative comments every single day but they won't go anywhere, which means they are still reading what you have to say.

What to Do With Negativity

So I like to let people have their say and I don't ban or block negative comments unless they become threatening or hateful. So what do I do when someone says something that is sure to rub people the wrong way?

I get to the root of the problem. They may say it in the worst and rudest possible manner, but there is a concern in there somewhere, so thank them for bringing it up and then address the issue at hand. Don't come back with an equally petty response (no matter how much you want to), because it will only encourage and egg on further comments like that one. Plus, it looks unprofessional (this is your site, remember).

If someone says something truly profane or hateful, you can edit it slightly to make it fair game for other responders, but don't delete it. That's content and content is valuable, no matter what it says. Plus, it's a slippery slope from deleting a negative comment to deleting anything that disagrees with your view point, and people will notice when this happens.

I understand how you feel. It's never fun to logon and see that someone so strongly disagrees with you that they would use profanity to describe it and ensure everyone else sees their opinion. But it's good for your blog and it often represents a real opinion, so respond to it in kind.

106

My 10 Secrets to Driving Comments with Content

I've been doing this for a long time - a *very* long time in fact. So long that I could probably drive comments within a week of starting a new blog, even if people didn't know it was me writing the content.

How do I do it? How do I get 20+ comments on a blog post within a week? Here are a few tips I use to convince people to share their thoughts with the group without resorting to cheap tricks:

1. **Ask for Them** - The easiest way to get comments is to ask for them. Every piece of content should have some kind of call to action at the end. Read another post, contact you, or leave a comment among them. So end your posts with a call for opinions on whatever you have been writing about. People respond to these.

2. **Mention Other Sites** - Mention other sites and other blogs in your comments. If nothing else, you will often get responses from those blog owners in your comments, and sometimes you will get more recommendations and comments from readers of those sites.

3. **State Your Opinion Clearly** - Be very clear in stating your opinion on a given topic. The stronger your opinion the more likely someone who disagrees with you will leave a comment saying so. This is a tricky one of course. The last thing you want to do is insult people on your site, so don't be controversial or forceful just to attract comments, but don't shy away from your opinions to avoid stepping on toes either.

4. **Don't Be Definitive** - One of the tricks to blogging is to write about a topic thoroughly enough to draw interest but not so much that your readers feel like they have nothing to add. When you write a blog post, think of ways you can

107

leave openings for your readers to engage with the site. Ask what types of things you want them to share and don't belittle potential opinions that people might share with you.

5. **Write Lots of Reviews** - Reviews are one of the quickest ways to get comments, because A) people are looking for them and B) people will often disagree with you. So, if your readers are interested in a particular topic, you can bet that a well written review will strike home with them.

6. **Respond to Other Content** - Write a post in response to content on another site or in another popular online forum of

some sort. People respond to these types of opinions strongly.

7. **Engage in Comments** - When you receive comments, by all means respond to them as quickly as possible. If people see ignored comments, they will be much less likely to leave a comment of their own.

8. **Integrate Facebook Commenting** - I don't do this but I see a lot of sites do it to varying levels of success. Facebook comments can be integrated directly into your blog posts, creating a piece of content on Facebook and having your readers comment on it directly there. The result is instant sharing but it can alienate any users without Facebook accounts.

9. **Reward Comments** - When people comment on your content, think of ways to reward them for their input. You can do this by calling them out in the next blog post or by writing posts in response to their comments. You can even hold comment contests asking for answers that you will then integrate into future posts.

10. **Built your posts around comments** - Finally, make sure you go through comments every now and then and create posts from them. Question and

answer posts are a great way to do this, but you can also just create a post using the responses you get. You might get some great ideas this way.

There are other strategies of course. You can intentionally offend people, write controversial reviews or stances on topics that will either infuriate or drive loyalty in your audience, you can pick already hot topics like Apple vs. Android or you can simply cheat and comment on your own posts, but I don't like these strategies. Forget the fact that they are often unethical and mask the real status of your blog - they water down and diminish the content on your site to such a point that the people you really want commenting will wander off.

You want a lively discussion - people who engage and are interested in prolonging your posts, not spewing angry commentary about whatever you write. To drive that kind of interest, you need to be willing to (and capable of) engaging people actively. It may take more time, but it's well worth it in my opinion.

Moderating All that Content

Today you have a blog with less than a dozen posts and maybe one or two comments if you are lucky. Maybe you haven't even started writing yet and are just absorbing as much information as possible before you press "Go!"

Whatever the case, you're going to be knee deep in blog posts and the comments that go with them in a matter of weeks, and then arises the issue of moderation. How do you keep track of everything you've written, what other people have written about those posts and what new topics you can cover that are unique to your site? It's not easy, especially if you start trying to track it later instead of right away.

Create an Early Plan

As early as possible (i.e. right now) start writing down the post titles and categories you have covered. Evernote is a good tool for this as you can organize your posts into notebooks and then easily search for topics to see what you've covered. Sure, you can search your blog and see if you've written about a given topic, but you don't always have Internet access and the last thing you want to do is start writing about something you already covered 9 months ago.

Second, you should set your blog to notify you of every new comment you receive. Unless your blog turns into the next Huffington Post or Boing-Boing, you won't receive more than 20 or 30 comments per post (probably per week) and it's very feasible that you could manage all of those yourself. If you get lucky enough to create the next mega-successful blog, hire someone to moderate for you.

Third, make sure you periodically review your blog posts, comments and any other content on your site to ensure editorial consistency. Once you have a loyal readership, you'll be surprised just how fast someone will call you out if you write a scathing review of a product only to come back three months later and say you love it. Inconsistency can kill a blog because it ruins your authenticity. Yes, you're in this to make money, but if people think you are manipulating your content to do so, you'll lose readers fast.

Comment Moderation Can Get Tricky

I have a very simple comment policy.
I don't want people to be discouraged from commenting on my site, ever. It's bad policy, but it's also bad policy to spend 90% of my time sorting through comments that I don't want on my site.

So I make sure Akismet is installed and active and that it is updated at all times. I also make sure to immediately review all comments that come in, and I make it possible for someone to post a comment automatically if they have already commented on the site or have registered.

Every comment still goes to my inbox, however, so that I can read it and ensure that it fits the rules of the site. I don't want someone going off the rails (or a third party to hack a user's account and start spamming the site). It's bad business and it can disrupt existing conversations on the site quickly.

Coming Up with Ideas When You Have None

Let's say you have set aside a chunk of time every week to sit down and write as many blog posts as you can. That time is pretty big but it is limited. So, when you sit down and whip out your thinking cap only to find that it's missing a few connections, it can be frustrating.

This is a problem I've faced more than a few times - the writer's block conundrum. If you write every day, you might consider taking a few hours or a day off from writing blog posts (there are other things you can work on in the interim) and let your brain process the day, but if you have limited time or if you really want to write *right now* then there are a few things you can do to jump start the writing process. Here are some of the things I do to come up with good blogging topics.
commentary of your own, this is a value-packed way to expand the content

* **Check Comments** - Step one is ALWAYS to check your comments. Comments are generally questions, clarifications or extensions of your posts so they often have tons of good ideas in them for posts. You should be reading your comments every day anyway, so jot down ideas while you read.

111

* Check Other Blogs - There are millions of other blogs out there so make sure you are reading at least a few of them to see what other people in your niche are writing about. Look for hot topics (we cover this earlier in the book) that you can weigh in on, or write reaction posts to other hot posts from other bloggers. You have an opinion; find hot topics and write about them. You can also gather links from other blogs and create a post that curates them into one place, or you can write about a topic with links to other sites littered throughout the content - I call this speedlinking.

* Updating Old Posts - My site has more than 1,000 blog posts on it to date. So, if I really cannot find a new post idea to write about, I can always go back to the archives, find an existing post and update it for today's audience. Trust, me no one is going to notice if you rework an article you wrote five years ago about the differences between Google and Yahoo! or something else that has changed substantially in that time.

* Check Other Input - Just like you got ideas through the comments on your site, consider checking your email as well. If you have a contact form, use that to solicit ideas or questions, and if people simply contact you via email (or Facebook/Twitter), then check there and get good ideas from people.

* Twitter Search - Do a quick hashtag search on Twitter for topics related to yours. You'll find thousands of tweets often directly or very closely related to whatever you've been writing about recently. Start writing them down.

* YouTube - You can always just take a video from YouTube, post it on your site and then write up a commentary on that video. It should, of course, be related to your niche and have interesting content for your readers, but as long as you add some solid on your site.

These are all highly effective ways to generate content ideas for your site, but with a little forward thinking, you can avoid ever having to worry about running out of ideas in the first place.

In most cases, you're going to spend plenty of time checking comments, perusing YouTube or checking other blogs in your niche, so whenever you see something you could write about, jot it down. Create a centralized list on your phone or in Evernote and then you can reference it anywhere when you need a new idea for a post. Simple as that.

Chapter Five:
List Building

If you're an Internet marketer in any sense of the word - even if all you've ever done is read a handful of posts on the Warrior Forum - you are familiar with list building. List building is the process of creating an email list and then encouraging people to subscribe and follow along as you provide tips and strategies or updates about your site.

The basic idea is that you bribe someone into joining your list and then you have carte blanche to promote just about anything you want to them.

Of course, there are caveats to this. If you literally promote whatever you want, it won't take long before those people on your list start clicking the "spam" or "unsubscribe" button when they see your name pop up in their inbox. This is not good - you need them to read your emails or there was no point getting them on the list in the first place.

So your list needs to be built around the same principles as your blog - value, value, value.

The goal here is not to send everyone on your list an advertisement every three days, but to provide them with supplemental value whenever they get those emails. Not only does this convince them to read your emails, but it can drive them back to your site where they'll eventually click on affiliate links, ads or other promotional tools you use on your blog.

So, what does a list for a blog need to include? What content will you eventually write for your subscribers, and how do you drive traffic to it and then back to your blog? Let's take a closer look.

The Three Step Process

Creation of a list involves three steps:
Step 1 - Bribe People to Join Your List
Step 2 - Provide Valuable Information Regularly
Step 3 - Call Them to Action

The most successful lists are those that clearly outline all three steps *before* actually signing anyone up. Saying you will fill the list out later or figure out your strategy down the line is a sure way to end up with a handful of people on a list that never hear from you.

Step 1 - The Bribe

You can get someone to read your blog simply by writing a good post. The only investment they must make is time and they can duck out of that whenever they want to. There is no commitment. But when you ask someone to sign up for your email list, they must give you information - usually a name and an email address - and for that, you had better bring the goods.

Do not fall into the trap of thinking that people will want to freely give away that information because you write good posts or that you can phone in a freebie that will get them on board. People are savvy and they want to know that they are getting a good deal in exchange for their name and email address.

You need to sell the bargain to them, not the other way around.

So, when you start creating your list, ask what would make a good, eye-catching opt-in bribe. What would convince people to sign up for your list and hand over their contact info. Some people will have read your blog before and may give you what you ask for just because they like you, but others may be new to the site and some might actually land directly on your squeeze page, having never read your blog.

So, how do you convert those people?

You over deliver. Just like you do in every blog post you write, video you record or image you share, you go out of your way to create something so powerful and so interesting that people will eagerly join your list and be blown away by what you've so freely given.

Basically, you need to ask yourself "what could I actually sell to my readers?" Now create that product and give it to them for free in exchange for their email addresses.

Before you ask me why you wouldn't just sell the product instead, consider the value of one email address. Sure, you can sell something to someone, but what happens when you can contact someone on a weekly basis for weeks, months or even years to come? What happens when you create a powerful trust-based relationship with hundreds of people who will likely buy whatever you recommend to them?

That single sale opportunity turns into many, many sales opportunities and you don't have to do any more work to make it happen. You just need to invest a little bit more up front. The payoff takes a bit longer but will be that much bigger.

What a Good Freebie Looks Like

So, when the time comes to create a freebie for your blog readers or anyone else who happens to stumble upon your blog, consider what the people who find your site want most. What specific thing can you offer that would provide immense value to your readers, so much so that they will sign up for your list to get it?

There are a few options here. Consider any of the following:

* **Video Course** - A video course is a great way to engage people with content that has high perceived value without having to create an exceptionally high quality content. With video you get a bit of a pass. People will see 7-10 videos of 20+ minutes as being an exceptionally valuable freebie, while a 50 page eBook (which would probably take longer to write or more money to have written) is a common enough resource online. This works to your advantage. If you have the resources to do so, I highly recommend video courses, ideally spread out over multiple email messages.

* **Templates** - The actual nature of your freebies will depend almost entirely on your audience, but in some cases your niche may be tailor-made for free stuff. For example, if you write in the tech, website or make-money-online niches, you can give away templates for just about anything. Wordpress themes, site templates, fonts, free graphics - whatever you think your audience would benefit best from is a good fit here.

* **Free Tools** - This fits into the same vein as free templates. The idea being that you ask yourself "what is a big problem this audience has?" Now create a tool that solves the problem you define. It takes a lot less effort than you'd expect, especially considering how many other sites are out there. Web tools,

template creators, iOS and Android apps - whatever you can develop at a low cost that solves a very real problem for your audience is a good fit here.

* **Free Services** - On my site I offer a free Wordpress installation service. Not only does it tend to draw a lot of people to my lists (I actually use my older eBooks as freebies for my main email list, but the Wordpress installs create a list too), but it makes me some money as I recommend a monthly HostGator plan to anyone that signs up for a free Wordpress site. The result is a $100 commission for anyone who takes me up on it - which is a higher percentage than you'd expect.

* **Free eBook** - This is how I get the vast majority of people on my site to join my email list. The free eBook in question is one I wrote a few years ago that compiled some of my best blog posts on various topics into an easy to read, 60 page format. It does quite well at converting new and recently returning visitors into subscribers on my email list.

* **Insider Information** - There is always the promise of free insider information too. This works better in some niches than others. For example, if you are in a financial niche that relies heavily on timely information, you can build a list by offering stock or Forex trading tips in the inboxes of your readers each day - something that few are qualified for and fewer still can afford to do.

Your biggest tool right now is information. You have a lot of it to offer, so make sure you are freely giving whatever you have available away. As a great marketer once said, ask yourself what your best product is. Now give it away for free. The single best thing you have to offer should go out as the bait on the hook.

Don't hold back the good stuff - hold back the dressing that will get people to come back later.

Before we jump into step two, let's take a closer look at how this works. Here is my site:

Notice how I have included a freebie opt-in at the top right corner that allows users to sign-up for my email list in exchange for the free book? It works quite well.

I also have a popover that shows up when someone has been on my site for a long enough period of time.

In both cases, I'm offering them something valuable that they will probably want. Why? Because it is the only way to ensure they feel suitably encouraged to sign up when they could just as easily subscribe to the RSS feed or bookmark the site.

You must come up with something similar and then find a way to sell it to your audience in an engaging way.

Step 2 - Provide Valuable Information Regularly

Just getting someone on your list is only step one. Heck, it's only half of step one, because after they join, they need to confirm their subscription and open a couple of your emails.

So when you reach step two, you have some work to do. You want these people to not only stay on your list but to engage with it actively, follow your recommendations and return to your site over and over again to read your content there, where the ads are. Remember, RSS is great, but not perfect because it doesn't house the ads.

So once you have someone on your list, your number one job is to ensure they stay there. This is where you need to whip out those value adding strategies you used to create the content on your site in the first place.

Think for a second about email lists that you belong to. Ask yourself two questions.

1. Which lists do you enjoy being a part of?
2. Which lists have you unsubscribed from or put on your spam list?

Those are two very different responses and most lists fall into the second camp or a limbo in between where they are not quite annoyed enough to click spam or unsubscribe but rarely, if ever, open that email. You don't want that.

You want them to open your email, read your message, think "damn, this guy is super helpful" and then visit your blog.

That's why we need to provide killer content on a regular basis.

The Content Magnet

Want someone to visit your site? Show them what they're missing. A weekly roundup of blog posts with a couple of bonus freebies can really drive people to visit your site, even if they prefer email and RSS.

The key here is consistency. Every week, send out an email that contains a list of everything you've done the previous week. Send it at the same time and with the same format every week. Include a list of posts, any videos you created, and any other appearances you had on other sites.

If a big event pops up or something happens that you want to share with your list, you can send out a new email in between, but that weekly roundup is set in stone.

Reprint and Enhance!

Another strategy that works quite well is to send out emails whenever you post a new blog entry. This only really works if you write less than 3-4 blog posts per week. Too many emails and people will get annoyed, even if you are sending them things they want.

Of course, if you want to reprint a blog post and send it out, find ways to enhance it. Give people a reason to open those emails other than to check your blog (which they can do just as easily by visiting your site or subscribing through RSS or Facebook). Add some extra content, reply to comments and questions or add some extra links from outside sites that will help you reach out to people on those sites.

Other Great Content

Last but certainly not least, you can put out a whole lot of other content to you list. Send them supplemental emails that include content that is not on your blog. New posts, webinars, free reports or videos, or anything else that you are creating or want to run by people before sending to others.

The goal of all this is not to bribe your list any further (they're already subscribed, right?). It's to create a relationship with them based on trust. They need to trust that you will provide reliable content filled with value and not just a bunch of sales pitches strung together trying to get them to buy something from your site.

Step 3 - Call them to Action

This is where you start making your move. Think of it this way. When you watch TV, you know you're going to see commercials.

A lot of them.
In fact, every 6-8 minutes there is a commercial break that lasts upwards of 3-5 minutes. For every 21 minutes of programming, there are 9 minutes of commercials. That's a lot of ads - almost a 2:1 ratio.

But you don't care because you get to watch a show that you like, and if you don't want to buy something, you just ignore that ad. We've become very good as a society at ignoring ads.

Your subscribers will do the same.

Hopefully not the ignoring of your ad, but the part where they don't mind seeing an ad or a pitch of some kind attached to high quality content. You are providing them with super high quality content on a regular basis that they can trust and that they would probably have to pay for under other circumstances.

So if you mention a few products every now and then or try to encourage them to go back to your site and read a post there,I guarantee they won't hold it against you.

In fact, in most cases, they will probably trust that recommendation that much more because you've been giving them such good guidance in your other messages.

So don't let an opportunity pass you by. When you send an email loaded with content, it should contain at least one call to action. You might not do this in your blog posts every time but with emails, ALWAYS include a call to action. Here's why.

You don't know how many emails one person will read. If someone only reads one out of every five emails you send, it is very easy for them to miss a pitch. If you include a pitch in every message, they will see it no matter which message they read.

Simple enough.

The hard part is creating pitches and CTAs that work effectively without driving people away. Here is where you're going to have to be careful.

Too many email marketers send emails that look like this:

Are you ready to upgrade your blogging prowess? Then you need to check out JohnChow.com, the Internet's leading site for building, growing and making serious cash with your blog.

Turn your hobby into a full time living and learn how you can become a top thought leader in the world of online marketing once and for all with John Chow's insider insights.

That's a hard sale and it's what you'll see on commercials, billboards and in radio ads. You want something softer - a gentle reminder that you have their back and want to help.

Have you ever listened to a podcast or a radio show and heard an ad being pitched by the show's host. It's usually personalized to some degree. The host describes how they benefit from the service, why they are recommending it and what you should do next.

It's still a pretty strong pitch, but it's coming from a place of deep trust. Presumably the company advertising paid a lot more money to get that kind of an ad placement on a popular show, but they probably get their money's worth too - it will convert MUCH better because it's personalized.

Here's how the hard sell above will look when softened and personalized:

Blogging isn't easy. I've been doing it for a few years and I can tell you this, anything that gives you an edge is worth checking out. So, if you haven't yet, or if you want to get some content ideas or strategies to grow out your blog a bit faster, check out JohnChow.com - one of my favorite sites online.

Do you see the difference?

The first reads like an infomercial. It hits on key reasons why you need to check out this site, asks you to think about your problem and then drives home what you can do to solve that problem.

The soft sell is personalized. It talks about the writer's problems and why the site was helpful to them. It doesn't push the issue. It just says "if you have this problem like me, this site will probably help." You still need to include a clear benefit statement in your pitch, otherwise it will perform poorly, but it doesn't need to be done in that Billy Blanks voice - it can be subtle and personal and it will be at least as effective without undermining the value of your list.

Of course, not every CTA needs to be a pitch. You run a blog, not an eCommerce site. That means you have a lot of options in this regard. A CTA can do any of the following:

* **Send Someone Back to Your Blog** - Remember where you placed all of those ads? They're not sitting in your emails, so you need people to get out of their inbox and back to your site. That's where you'll convert that traffic into cash in your pocket.

* **Send Someone to Another Email List** - A highly effective way to drive traffic to your site is to perform ad swaps with other list owners. An ad swap is when you send out a message that promotes the list of someone else and they do the same for you. Don't send a hard sell for their list - just include a strong CTA at the end of one of your normal emails that convinces people to visit their site.

125

* Get Them to Signup for a Webinar - A webinar is an easy-to-produce product that has a strong value add for your followers. Consider creating a webinar open only to the people on your list, or hold a Google+ Hangout and invite your closest followers, such as your subscriber list.

* Ask for Their Opinion in a Survey - When I'm developing a new product or trying to figure out what to write about for a new product or service, I often ask my readers. One way to do this is to create a survey with a service like SurveyMonkey and ask the people on your list to fill it out. You'll be surprised how quickly the response pans out.

* Get them to Follow on Facebook or Twitter - This is the simplest CTA you can pitch and it works quite well. The more places you are in contact with your followers, the more opportunities you have to ensure they read your posts and click your ads. So, get them on Facebook and Twitter whenever possible.

* Buy Something - Listen, if you create a list of buying leads - people who have already bought something from you, you can send them a few more ads with actual purchase links in them. But for people on your blog - people who are up until now only interested in reading your posts - these should be few and far between. That doesn't mean you can't pitch people on sales opportunities. It just means it shouldn't be the core of what you do.

That's a short list too. Imagine all of the things you have to offer and what you want your audience to do. You can pitch any of those things to them on your site. Keep in mind too that there is a double bonus from having them revisit your site.

Google tracks repeat visitor rates. Higher rates mean better SERPs in the long term because it means you are providing extra value to those visitors. It should be a part of your regular SEO strategy to encourage revisits and this is a great way to do it.

Strategies to Build Your List

If you've spent more than 10 minutes on the big Internet marketing blogs or forums (including mine), you've probably noticed a lot being written about list building - how it is the most effective way to make money online and how it can be the backbone of any business, even if you get slapped something fierce by Google.

All of that is true, but it applies a little differently to a blog.

Your demographic is broader than a site devoted to selling things and your pitch is more complex than "buy this!" You are selling ideas and content, not products or services, and that means your list building strategies must be better integrated into your site's purpose.

I want to go through a few of the strategies I use for list building, what other site owners use, and how all of these can be tweaked to fit your audience.

The Squeeze Page

A squeeze page is exactly what it sounds like - a landing page on your site with absolutely no outside links - a page designed solely to get someone to sign up for your list. It is immensely simple and works effectively with or without a freebie (though much better with one).

Squeeze pages are often more effective on sites that have a sales component to them. A blog benefits from high page view rates and your freebie offer is in their face constantly and can even be integrated into your posts at certain points, so a dedicated squeeze page is not necessary in every instance. But it can still work. More importantly, it can capture people who are not convinced by the other things on your site. As it stands, the traditional blog has the following two capture methods:

1. Sidebar Opt In
2. Popover Opt In

The former is often ignored by people who assume everything over there is an ad. You can handle part of this preconception by integrating a video to introduce it, but even then, a lot of people will just go to the posts.

The second is more effective, especially if you time it just right so the popover only appears after a few seconds of reading. But even then, there are people who reflexively close anything that pops up on the page. They've either been hard coded to close pop ups from the days of Netscape and AOL, or they are reading and don't want to stop.

In either case, it doesn't mean they aren't interested. It just means they haven't fully considered the opportunity you're offering.

So we give them a third option - a squeeze page.
The squeeze page should be linked to at the top of your site (it can be in a submenu if you don't want it to be prominent). Here's what I do:

Did you enjoy this post? Get John Chow Dot Com updates via email...

Stay up to date with all of John Chow's tips for making money online and blog posts by subscribing via email. Your email will be kept private and never shared with anyone.

| Enter your email address... | Subscribe via Email |

I respect your privacy. You may unsubscribe at any time with just one click.

You can then link to this page from any of your posts. This is effective if you are discussing something directly related to the freebie you are giving away. Don't over sell it or it will seem that your blog exists solely to convert people to your list. But don't undersell it either - there are a lot of opportunities here.

The Headline

Your headline is the most important part of the page. I'm a firm believer that if you create a video in which you don't stare at your feet or have a Hitler t-shirt on you'll do okay. People are always impressed by someone who appears authentic in a video (i.e. don't sound like a used car salesman). But for them to click play on your video, you must first create a headline that convinces them to start watching.

A squeeze page headline should do three things.

1. Introduce a Problem
2. Introduce a Solution
3. Define the Terms

So your headline will contain three simple clauses that can have a profound impact on your reader, and since you know your audience better than anyone, this should be easy.

129

That's a simple headline but it's effective, and with a few tweaks and some split testing I'll bet I can hit 20% conversion on this page in no time flat.

Remember, the goal is not to tell your readers what your page does, but to describe to them why they should care. Most people could care less about a product's features. They want to know what's in it for them.

The Video

Lest I completely oversimplify the video, there are a few things you should do to ensure this is effective.

First, remember that this is your blog and you're already putting your name out there. So there is no good reason not to be on that video yourself unless you have severe stage fright. The highest conversion rates will always come if you show up on screen and say "hey, thanks for reading, sign up for more cool stuff".

If you are uncomfortable doing this, however, there are a lot of good ways to get around it. The simplest strategy is to create a quick PowerPoint presentation and then record your voice over the top of it. At the very least you should include at least some voiceover to personalize the page a bit.

I aim for between 45 and 90 seconds for this type of video. The longer it is, the less likely your readers will stick around and see the whole thing, so get to the point fast and be thorough. If you were stuck in an elevator with someone who wanted to know about your list before you reached your floor, what would you say? That's what should go into your video.

The Opt In

Last but not least is the opt in form. This is about as simple as it gets since any autoresponder service you use will have a tool in place that automates form creation. Here's what it looks like using my service of choice, Aweber.

Ad Swaps and Solo Ads

A squeeze page works if you can drive traffic to that page. However, if you don't yet have the traffic coming into your blog to do that or if you are wary of pestering your small readership to get people on a mailing list, consider these other methods to generate list subscribers fast.

Email marketing through other lists is a very simple process and works exceptionally well if you have a good freebie to promote. There are two options here - barter or cash.

To barter your list, you need to have a list in place to start. For the most part, you need at least 100 subscribers for this to be an option. The goal is to swap your list with another list owner in your niche. You each mail each other's subscribers and offer the freebie (using your squeeze page) and voila, your list grows.

Plus, you're offering your list members free stuff from other lists that you like. This works effectively in small bursts (but should be limited, since even good freebies can overwhelm your list if you send them out every few days).
That's an ad swap, and if you are in the right niche, it is a very effective way to build your list fast.

The other method that works even faster is solo ad buys. The problem here is that solo ads cost money.

A solo ad means you're basically hiring someone to deliver a certain number of clicks to your site through a link in an email they send out on your behalf. Usually the cost will be between $0.20 and $0.50 per click. And that does not necessarily mean each person who clicks converts to a subscriber. You need a good squeeze page that converts well (hence my talking about it first), and the list you purchase an ad on should be active and interested in signing up for your type of offer.

Solo ads are very effective, as most good solo ad buys will convert between 20% and 50% of the people who click. That means that for every $20 you spend you will get between 5 and 50 new subscribers. You can probably expect a number closer to 10-20, but that's not too bad if you're eager to grow your list fast. The major downside is that you need some cash on hand to do this. So, if you're not monetizing that list immediately, you might want to wait.

Instant Monetization

Before you write off solo ads as a strategy that could never work for you, consider this quick and easy option to cover the cost of your ads.
I've done this and seen it done by others to great effect. It requires a fair amount of testing, but if you integrate it properly, it can result in some big time list gains quickly.

Step 1 - Create Your Squeeze Page

Create a squeeze page like normal. This is where you will drive traffic from the solo ads you purchase. Test it if you can with traffic from your blog or with a smaller solo ad before moving to step 2. You want to tweak it if possible to improve your conversion rates before you start trying to monetize that traffic.

Step 2 - Create a Thank You! Page

When someone signs up for your list, most autoresponders offer an option for a redirect after confirmation. They will receive an email after signing up asking them to confirm their subscription. This is an anti-spam tool and is required in the US and a handful of other countries to protect privacy.

Once they have confirmed, you can send them to a new page saying "thanks for signing up!" This is where the magic happens. Ideally, this page should include instructions for retrieving your freebie, but we can add something else there as well.

Step 3 - Sell Something!

Instead of just thanking your new subscriber for giving you their email address, place a quick pitch on this page for a product you think they will like. This can be done in a number of ways. You can either create a sales page if you have something you want to sell, or you can simply place a quick ad for an affiliate product you are promoting.

As your blog ages, you can even link to a few of the products you have reviewed recently. One thing that I like about Amazon is that on every single page of the checkout process, from adding something to your cart, to downloading a sample Kindle book to actually buying something, they are saying "how about this too?" while flashing a star rating at you to help you make the choice.

You can do the same on your blog, and it's almost guaranteed you'll see people clicking on those links and possibly even buying those items.

How does this pay for solo ads?

Think of it this way. If your solo ads convert at a 30% rate (a good number but not exceptionally high), that means you are paying roughly $1 for ever new subscriber you get to your list.

That might seem like a lot of money, but what if you can convert 5% of those new subscribers to buy a product you've promoted on your blog at some point? And what if that sale results in a commission of $27? Then you are making a profit as long as you convert at least 1 in 25 people to buy something.
It's not a fortune, but it's free list building.

It will take some tweaking. Almost universally it doesn't work right away, so DON'T start spending money on this until you are sure it will convert. But when it does start converting, it's a great way to build a list on autopilot.

Freebie Promotions

One of the quickest and biggest "bang for your buck" ways to generate leads to your list is to create a sales page (a bigger and badder version of your squeeze page), and send people there with active promotions.

You can do this in a number of ways. You can pay people money for each lead they send to that page or you can purchase a WSO on the Warrior Forum or equivalent forum ($40 in most cases) and drive traffic that way. In the case of the latter, you'll usually get between 50 and 200 subscribers from one $40 WSO fee - if you use the forum a lot you'll get even more over time.

This is not necessarily the most time effective way to build your list, but if you need a quick surge of subscribers so you can start performing ad swaps, it will give you that surge.

The Importance of a List

If your head is spinning, let's take a step back real quick and
think about what a list is really for. What does this list do and why is it so important to have one?

Even if you do nothing I've outlined above and simply place an opt-in form on your site and ask people to sign up in exchange for free stuff, you're creating a method by which you can contact them whenever you want.
Most of the Internet revolves around convincing someone to come to you - list marketing (and social media in some instances) is based on going to them and finding as many effective methods of doing so as possible.

So, don't miss this opportunity. Convert that traffic into people coming to your site and I guarantee you'll be happy with the results.

Chapter Six:
Monetizing 101

This is what you came for, isn't it? The big chapter (the longest in the book in fact) about making money with your blog. Before we get started I want to encourage you to go back and read through the first few sections if you haven't yet done so.

Yes, if you already have a blog, this section will be immensely powerful for many of you. But even for veteran bloggers there is a lot of good stuff in the first few chapters that you might find interesting.

With that said, let's take a look at my formula for cashing in on your blog .

Blogs = Cash

Think for a moment about what a blog is and how it works. A blog is a massive collection of content that creates loyal readers that return to your site again and again to read whatever new posts you have written, watch your videos and contribute to the conversation. If you play your cards right, you can tank upwards of 10-15 page views *per visitor* per month. They're not Facebook numbers, but as far as a website anyone can build goes, it's damn good.

So when you create a big enough blog with enough readers and update them with fresh, interesting content on a regular basis, you have a petri dish primed for monetization.

In simpler terms, traffic is valuable and your blog will get a LOT of traffic. So, the goal then is to create a system that cashes in on that traffic as effectively as possible.

This is, of course, easier said than done. There are dozens of bloggers that have approached me with four, five or even six figure monthly traffic numbers that could not figure out how to turn all those eager readers into cash in their pockets.

And this isn't a mere issue of greed. These sites are expensive to operate. When you have 100,000 visitors to your site every month and they each look at 10+ pages, plus a good 10,000 of them sign up for your autoresponder list, that's a lot of bandwidth. You're looking at a good $200+ per month for the hosting account and $100+ for the autoresponder service. It adds up, so even if you blog only for the fun of it, you want to make at least a little bit of money to cover your expenses.

Thankfully, the strategies I'm about to show you will do MUCH more than just cover your basic expenses.

First, let me tell you my story.

Here is what my blog looked like in 2007 when I started showing people how I grew my site:

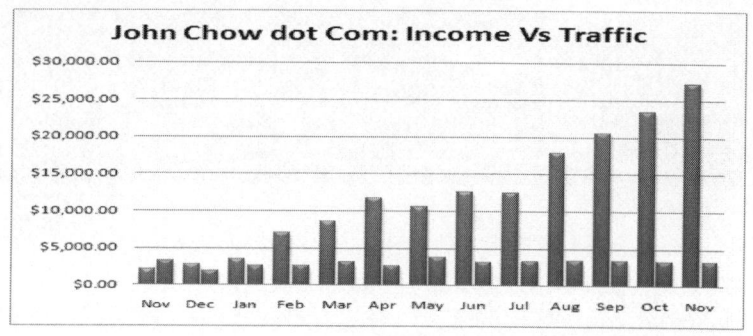

137

As you can see, it took only one month to go from spending more than I made to making more than I spent. By the end of 1 year, I was making 10 times as much as I spent.

But this was 2007 and I didn't start in 2007. I started in 1999 creating a website about a computer I was building. I didn't make money for a long time. I played around and tested things and started building my site, TechZone shortly after that.

It wasn't pretty:

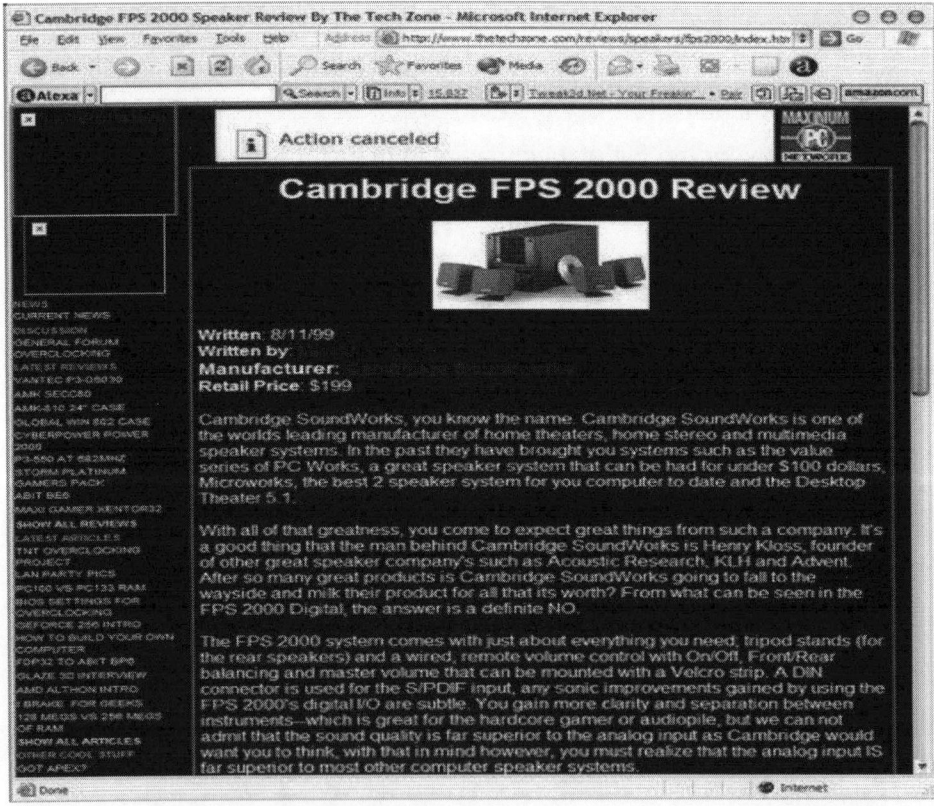

But I kept at it and that site grew fast, becoming a mega traffic source over the course of a few years. The dotcom bubble burst decimated my income, but I kept at it, using what I had learned to revamp and restart my site using the new Google ads network in 2003. I knew what to do then, and you can read about it in this book.

I started my personal blog with future profit in mind and the site thrived both because of and in spite of that. You can do the same, but first, you're going to need to lay some ground work.

Create an Editorial Plan

Every good business needs editorial guidelines that dictate what you are and are not willing to do within the context of your mission. What I mean is, if someone contacted you tomorrow offering $1,000 a month to post a pornographic ad on your site, would you say yes?

The vast majority of you would not and the answer would be simple. But not all opportunities are as cut and dry as porn vs. no porn. What about Google AdSense? What about sponsored posts? What about popover ads? What about guest posts and joint ventures?

These are all things that can all make you money, but you need to decide early which of them you are willing to pursue and which of them fit your editorial plan. The vast majority of readers will not only accept but support your efforts to monetize - we all have to make a living right? But don't push their patience too far - the last thing you want is to alienate loyal readers because they grow tired of the ads all over your site or don't approve of the types of ads you post.

Here are some questions you should ask yourself before monetizing any components of your site:

* What types of products or services will benefit your readers?
* What would you be annoyed at if it were on another site you used?
* How many total ads are on your site? How many are you willing to place?
* Would you personally vouch for the product you are promoting to your readers?
* Do the ads make your site look different? Bad? Interesting?
* How much management are you willing to do over advertising?

These are all factors that can impact the types and scope of advertising used on your site.

Affiliate Marketing

To me, the most powerful form of advertising is the kind that is personalized to my audience. If you look at my site, you'll find a number of examples of this. But far and away the most powerful (and effective) method I've used to date is affiliate marketing.

Affiliate marketing is very simple (and it makes amazing use of the list you created in the last chapter). Essentially, what you do is drive traffic to an information product created by a product vendor, and if a sale is made, you earn a commission on that sale.

What makes it such a profitable endeavor, however, is that those products often sell for $100 or more and the commissions are anywhere from 50% to 75% of the sale price. The reason is simple. Information products have very little or no overhead. There is no cost of printing or publication and the final product is still valuable because it contains incredibly useful information.

That is the key for me. A lot of bloggers will promote anything that converts well and has a high commission. I only promote those products that I personally feel will provide value to my readers. Specifically, what this means is that the product is something I would use and therefore feel would benefit my readers. My reviews are legitimate and honest and I never promote a product that I don't support.

This does two things. First, it ensures that people are much more willing to follow my recommendations. Second, it ensures that when they read my earnings disclaimer they don't care. There is a myth out there that when you tell someone a product you're promoting could make you money, they will walk away. But in reality, they just want to know you are looking out for them.

You don't walk away from a car salesman when he shows you the heated seats in a new sedan do you? Why would my readers leave because I show them a product I think they will like, even if I get a commission for promoting it?

Integrating Affiliate Marketing Into Your Blog

Affiliate marketing can be done in a number of ways. Like the content on your blog, you can just as easily phone it in as you can blow it out of the water. I want you to aim for the latter, so let's take a closer look at how the process works.

Step 1- Find a Product You Want to Promote

There are thousands upon thousands of products on the Internet that you can promote and make a fairly good commission from. If you've ever promoted information products before, you probably have a strategy in place already, but bear with me for a moment as I take a step back and show you how I go about it.

First, I ask myself what people in my niche, and specifically my readers, really need. What specific problems do they have? Don't just brainstorm - actually ask your readers. Check Google Analytics to see what search queries perform best on your site, check comments for frequent questions, check your inbox and contact form submissions and if you are still unsure, actually ask people to answer the question directly. The goal is to *know* what people on your site need from you. You can create content as a result that will fit those needs and subsequently recommend products that fulfill specific needs they may have.

The next step is to look for the best products in that particular category. They can be brand new, ten years old or in pre-release. The goal is to find the best - the ones that you would personally use and recommend. Get a review copy from the owner of that product (most of them will accommodate) or go back through the list of products you have actually used and would like to write reviews about.

Things NOT to Do

I see some affiliate marketing courses advising their students to go out and find the highest paying product in a particular niche. This is a bad strategy for a number of reasons. To start, you then focus more on your end payout than on helping your readers. Even from a financial standpoint this makes very little sense. Think about it like this. If you recommend a shitty product to your readers and they all buy it, what do you think their response will be when you recommend another product, even if it's pretty good?

Not only is it your responsibility to ensure that your readers trust you, you need to be able to back up any recommendations you make. Recommending a product you haven't used because it has a big payout is a one way ticket to a very short lived blogging career. You are a web-journalist and your opinion matters. Yes, you get paid for that opinion (which makes it a lot harder to consider yourself a journalist), but you should still hold to the highest possible levels of integrity in selecting products to promote and writing reviews of those products.

Finding Products

With all that in mind, the next step is to find your target products. There are a number of resources on which to do this. Here are a few of my favorite marketplaces and the benefits they offer:

* **Clickbank** - Clickbank is good for info products, mostly in non-IM categories. While there are plenty of IM products here, there are a few quirks that keep me away from them. Stick with niche products here - dog training, health topics, etc.

* **Amazon.com** - If you talk about, review or promote physical products, Amazon is the way to go. They have pretty much everything you can imagine for sale on the site in some form and it is incredibly easy to create promotional banners and text links.

* **Commission Junction** - Commission Junction features CPA offers such as insurance inquiries, Netflix and trial offers. This doesn't fit a lot of niches, but they pay out extremely well. You do need to apply to use this site, however.

* **Warrior Forum** - The Warrior Forum is an IM-only site for products related to making money online. The WSO section of the site is represented on

143

JVZoo.com and WarriorPlus.com, so if you're interested in promoting anything, look on those sites.

There are dozens more of course, including some vendors who don't use marketplaces at all, but directly contact potential affiliates and use a credit card processor on their own. Always review and check any new program to ensure it has been around for long enough to ensure quality. You want to know that the products offered on that site will convert when you make a sale and you get credit for it.

Step 2 - Read the Promotional Materials and Use the Product

Here's a step that a lot of marketers skip, probably in an effort to make money faster. Unfortunately, rushing this process will only ensure you make less money. Like all good things in life, the only way to ensure you actually succeed in making a decent profit with your marketing efforts is to do them properly, taking your time to ensure it is all done right. If you rush things, you are almost assured to have issues at some point in the process.

Fortunately, most vendors will make it as easy as possible to do this, knowing that you are the only link they have to getting their product to the masses. So, when you find a product you want to review, check the product's website and look for an "affiliates" section.

The site owner will provide a large number of resources to promote his product, including swipe emails, graphics, free reports and a bunch of other resources that will, ideally, make it quick and easy to create a portal through which to buy that product.

We only need to write a review, so the most important thing for me is that I have access to the product and that I can use a graphic or two of the product.

Not all affiliates make this easy, but in most cases, if you email or Skype the vendor and ask them for access to the product, they will give it to you.

Find the product you want to promote, jot down the email of its creator or affiliate manager and then send that email and nine times out of ten, you'll get a free copy to check out.

Step 3 - Write or Record a Review for the Product

Use the product.

Don't write a review until you have used the product. There are a few reasons for this. First, it's unprofessional. You're undermining the purpose of a review and undercutting your own credibility. Why would anyone trust you to provide them with reliable reviews if they think you're only going to make them up whenever it suits you to make money.

Second, it might be illegal depending on where you live. At the least it is disingenuous and at the most it is illegal. In the US, for example, it is illegal to write a review and post a testimonial for a product you have not used unless you clearly state you have not used it and did not get any results from it (and without that, good luck getting any clicks through your review).

It may take longer, but trust me, a well-researched review based on your personal experiences will have a HUGE impact on the effectiveness of your review.

When the time comes to write or record, outline a few things first. Especially if you plan on recording a review, you want to have a structure in place and not just wing it. Here are the things you'll want for your review:

1. Background of the product - What is it, what pre-conceptions do people have and why have you picked it up to review?

2. Clear definition of the problem it purports to solve - There is a specific problem the creators of this product have in mind when they sell it. What is that problem and which of your readers are affected by it?

3. List of things you like - Now, go into the things you like about the product. Sometimes I lead with an outline of the product and how I used it, but I always lead with the pros so I can keep people engaged.

4. List of things you don't like - Everyone has an internal voice repeatedly saying *"but?..."* when they read a review. They're waiting for that big "but?..." statement to dash their hopes of a good buy. This is where you give them what they expect. If it's a good review, explain why the "but?..."'s are not a good reason to bypass the product, and if it's a bad product, drive home how bad they are.

5. Your final verdict - Finally synthesize everything you've said into a single clear statement. It doesn't have to be "buy" or "don't buy". It might be "buy if you..." and "don't buy if you..." But make it clear what the reader should do. People read reviews to help them make buying decisions. So help them make a buying decision.

This is the general outline of a good review of a product that you hope to promote as an affiliate. Why are we going to tell people bad things about the product? Because the product is not perfect and there are undoubtedly problems with it that need to be discussed. On top of that, it isn't realistic to have zero problems with a product. If someone reads your review and sees that there is nothing at all wrong with the product, they either trust you and buy it, likely to find that you glazed over shortcomings, or they don't trust you and don't buy it at all.

146

Honesty and a careful analysis of all faults ensures that the reader of the review has realistic expectations - the most important motivating factor for them to purchase is still there - your endorsement.

Step 4 - Integrate that Review Content into You Blog

Once you create your review, it needs to go on your blog. This is the easy part - or is it? A lot of work goes into researching a product, writing or recording a review and preparing it for publication. So, make sure you publish at a time that will ensure maximum viewership. You want as many people as possible to see and interact with your review so that there is a larger chance of making sales of that product.

So it's time for more footwork. Check the following before posting your review:

1. Your Current Content Calendar - Check your content calendar and make sure there are not any overlaps. Don't launch two reviews too close to each other. Don't post a review next to an editorial that could contradict something in your review. Don't post back to back videos (unless you do a lot of video content on your blog). You get the idea.

2. When You Get the Most Traffic - Check Analytics to see when you get the most readership to your site. You want to post when you know the largest number of eyeballs will see it. Check for the time they arrive and what days of the week have the biggest surge in traffic. Weekends are usually slow, but not for every niche, so analyze carefully before choosing.

3. Whether Other Reviews are Live - Look for other reviews written by bloggers in your niche. Try not to post your own review a day or two after another major review has garnered a lot of attention - it is quicker to be ignored or written off. Don't wait too longer either, and if no other reviews are up, get yours up right away - you could get the first wave of traffic for those review terms.

4. Special Promotions from the Vendor - If the vendor is having a launch sale, is giving away freebies as part of the launch or is helping out affiliates with special promotional bonuses, time your review launch accordingly and integrate those things into the review.

5. Your Email List Sequence - You're going to want to tell people on your list about your review. This is a great way to drive traffic from your list to your monetized posts without it seeming like a sales pitch. Just tell people that you wrote a review and are excited about it - the rest will happen on its own. But make sure not to send the message out on a previously scheduled broadcast day. You can't stop all overlaps since every subscriber is on a different schedule, but you can minimize the risk of sending out three messages in less than 24 hours.

These five factors can all determine, or at least influence when it is best to post your own review. Just throwing something up online is not enough - it needs to be carefully timed and launched to fit the behaviors of both your site and your audience.

Step 5 – Follow-up with Your Readers

Last but not least, follow-up. A review is great, but it may not be seen by everyone. Or maybe they put it on their to do list and then buy the product through a different affiliate link. You need to stay fresh in people's minds to capture anyone who didn't get or follow your first links and to recapture anyone that was partially interested but forgot or decided to wait. You can do this in one of a few ways, including:

* Social Media - Post your review on Facebook and Twitter and you can easily followup in a couple of days to remind people that you wrote a review and that they should check it out.

* Email List - Send a broadcast to your email list when you first write your review and then another broadcast when you want them to followup and check it again. Don't send them too close together and make sure you include a good reason to do it - make people feel like they are benefiting by reading that review.

* New Blog Post - You can always put up a new blog post reminding people to check your last one, or you can mention it offhandedly in future blog posts and link to the review you wrote before. Even a quick one-sentence mention in reference can boost sales by as much as 5-10%.

* Ads on the Site - You can be blunt too and simply post a few ads on your site. Banner ads work well to remind people of a review they read, or you can put a popover on your home page reminding people to check the review. I choose not to do this most of the time except for products I really like or that convert very well, but it can be effective depending on your audience.

If you follow these five steps carefully, not only will your reviews have a bigger and better impact, but people will eagerly look forward to reading about the products you promote. They will look for more information from you before making a buying decision and ultimately, you will have a great deal of editorial and commercial power in your niche.

Affiliate Links on Your Site

Like I said, you can promote an affiliate product in a number of ways. I often choose to do so with reviews posted on my blog. You can also promote products with banner ads, webinars and list mailings (as mentioned above). In each case, you need to provide a link for people to click that will give you credit for the referral.

That's why Wordpress is so powerful. There are simple, yet easy tools you can use to track your referrals in Wordpress.

* LinkTrackr
* WP Wizard Cloak
* PrettyLinkPro
* LinkHopper

Simply enter in your custom URLs and your hoplink and your readers will be redirected toward the sales page of whatever product you have produced without realizing it is an affiliate link (or without being fully conscious of it in any case).

Specific Tools

Affiliate marketing is a powerful tool for bloggers. It combines the trust-loyalty nature of a blog with the high dollar value return of information marketing. In my opinion, there is no better way to earn money with a blog than to promote top dollar products in your niche that you support.

However, because affiliate marketing is so powerful, there are a number of tools available for it – some of them amazing and others much less so. Here are some of my favorites in a number of categories, including sites where you can find products to promote:

Recommended Affiliate Marketing Tools

1. **Link Trackr** – If you want to track anything – from keywords being clicked on your site to banner ad impressions, this is the tool to use. The cost is low to start which is great since most blogs won't need to track too many links right away and it provides the kind of data needed to sell advertising on your site.

2. **Market Samurai** – This is the biggest and best market research tool on the Internet. It provides not only in-depth keyword and niche discovery tools but is constantly updated with recent algorithm changes and anything else that might affect your niche.

3. **Keyword Elite** – Another very powerful keyword research tool. If you want to know which terms will sell when advertising in Google or selling advertising, this is the tool you need to find out.

Recommended Affiliate Marketing Networks

1	Clickbooth.com
2	Clickbank.com
3	Neverblue.com
4	affiliate.com
5	Crushads.com
6	amazon.com
7	cj.com
8	linkshare.com

Using These Tools to Make Money

When using these tools, your goal is to make money, so you should focus primarily on what value you can offer your readers that will convert to cash down the line. This is a tricky balancing act.

When you create a simple website that focuses on a review or even just on funneling traffic to a product you want to promote, it takes very little time and you don't have to worry about your reputation – often your name isn't on the site.

But when you are building a blog that relies heavily on your name and your brand and the amount of time and energy you put into both, you want to know that the site will be successful because of your endorsements, not in spite of them.

So you need to be careful in your use of affiliate marketing networks and programs. Don't just throw up whatever tools you want to make money with. Use them carefully to promote the products you like.

Other Forms of Advertising on Your Blog

I'm going to clump a lot of the other monetization methods I use into one category, but these are all very different and can be used in various formats depending on what type of site you are running and what types of products you think your readers will want to use.

Before you place any ads on your site, however, remember that the goal of this is to provide *value* to your readers. They want to know that whatever you recommend will be useful to them. And while it is easy to think that a banner ad on your site is not a recommendation from you, that is not the case.

Anything on your site has your implicit backing. This is why I am so careful about what ads I allow on my site and how they are organized and presented, something I am extra careful about when it comes to Google Ads as you will soon see.

When you first start your blog, monetization will be sparse. In fact, I will show you in a short while that monetizing early doesn't often make sense - if only because the returns on investment will be so small and it can turn off a lot of early readers who don't yet know you.

That said, when your site reaches a certain point, you will have people quite literally breaking down your door asking for ad slots. Traffic converts to cash and people know that, no matter what niche you are in. So your job, to avoid this becoming an obnoxious problem you must deal with, is to clearly define where ads can and will be placed on your site and then solicit placement of those ads from the people whose products you support.

There are two ways you can do this - you can either join an ad network that will supply ads to you based on criteria you define, or you can place an ad asking for ads (ironic, no?) on sites like BuySellAds.com. Here are some of your options:

* **Media Selling** - If you go to a site like BuySellAds.com and do a quick search through the database there, you will see a large number of websites that are selling ad space. Each of them clearly defines the size and location of the ad space they are selling and assigns a price based on either the duration of the ad's appearance or a certain number of impressions. You can do any of this, but you must first define those factors. How much space will you set aside for ads, what slots are available and what will you charge? More on this in a bit.

* **Google AdSense** - The simplest and most often used (and abused) form of slot-based advertising on blogs is Google AdSense. Google's content-network-based advertising platform is both a blessing for small blogs and a curse for those who unwittingly place ads that don't reflect their products. I will

153

go into much greater depth on AdSense and when it works (and doesn't) later on, but for now keep in mind that it is only useful in certain situations.

* **Amazon Ads** - Amazon's affiliate program is a little different. While the payouts are relatively small (often between 4% and 8% depending on how many sales you drive) the selection is greater and you can promote quite literally anything that Amazon sells directly. That includes large, expensive products like fitness equipment and solar panels as well as software and movies. If your niche includes a lot of high dollar physical products, this is a big opportunity for you.

* **Banners from Affiliate Products** - You can also go to the sites of the products you are promoting with your reviews and get a banner ad that can be placed on your site. This is great if there is a product that is converting well or if you want to supplement a review you wrote last week. However, a banner slot is often more valuable when sold to a company directly or when matched to an affiliate program that you may not review, like a hosting company.

Your website, as it grows, is fertile land that increases in value with each bump in traffic. Don't let it sit idle when you could be reaping that soil for big returns. As soon as you reach the point where you are comfortable placing ads, take advantage of all that traffic and start monetizing.

Amazon Product Ads

One of the fastest growing forms of affiliate marketing is physical product marketing through the Amazon marketplace. There are a few reasons for this.

154

1. **It's Easy** - Amazon's Associate program is very easy to use and you can create an ad for any product sold on the site directly (there are third party products that don't always apply).

2. **Those Products Convert** - Amazon has spent billions of dollars tweaking their product pages and shopping cart experience to eke every cent they can out of a visitor. Other sites may convert, but Amazon will always convert better, which means more money in your pocket, even if commissions are lower.

3. **The World is Your Shopping Cart** - You can buy almost anything on Amazon, which means you can promote almost anything. Write reviews of sewing machines, mattresses, books or fitness machines - they all pay out.

4. **Huge Upsell Opportunities** - The reason you can make a big chunk of change on Amazon where the affiliate payout is usually 4% (up to 8% if you sell a lot of stuff), is that the number of people who buy multiple products on Amazon is very high, and even if you only promoted one product, you would get credit for everything in their cart at checkout - which means a formerly $3.75 commission could turn into a $40 commission quite easily.

What Google became for online search, Amazon has become for online commerce. When someone thinks to buy something online, they go to Amazon. Only if they can't find it there do they check another resource. So if you have a link to a product on your site that they might want and it goes to Amazon, the presale is already done - Amazon can do the rest, and if you present it right on your site (with a review or a themed blog post), you'll often get your point across and make a sale quite easily.

Defining and Charging for Ad Slots

The space on your blog grows exponentially in value as your site gets hits. More hits = more traffic per page and more impressions. More impressions

155

means more money per slot. But how do you define those slots on your site and what will you charge for them? Here are a few quick tips to help you do just this:

1. Designate Ad Space

Don't let yourself become *that guy* - the one who willy nilly sells any space on his site just to make a few bucks. Sit down and lay out exactly where you want ads to be placed. Look at other big sites in your niche and determine what is considered okay in your field. In some cases, you may only want a handful of 125x125 ads on the right side bar and in others you may sell space at the top, along the footer and across the side bar. It's up to you, but make sure you don't sell so much that you drive away your readership.

Here's what mine looks like. One big banner across the top and then a smaller sponsors section along the right side of the screen with square block ads. There are a few others on the site, but most of them are for my own services and products.

2. Look at Buy Sell Ads

There are a lot of ad networks. BuySellAds is just one of the largest and one that I happen to like it because it has an open marketplace that you can go to and search to see what other people are charging and how much ad space they are selling on their sites. Here's an example when I search for "make money online"

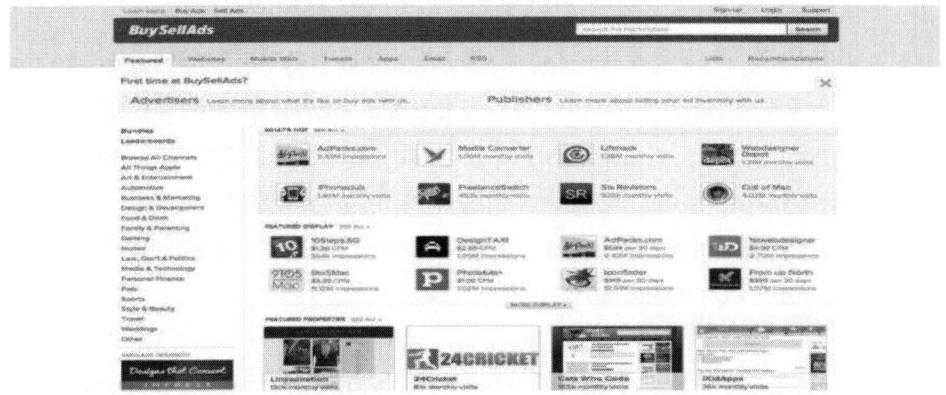

A few of them are not in my niche, but the largest of those that are have a variety of ad slots I can review and price mine against:

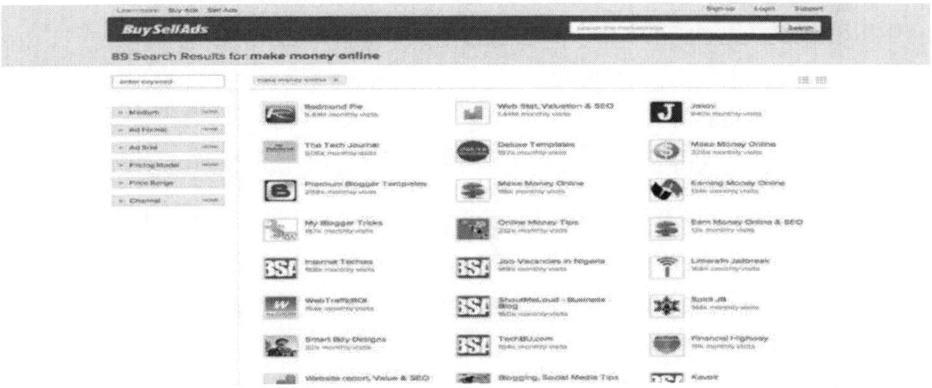

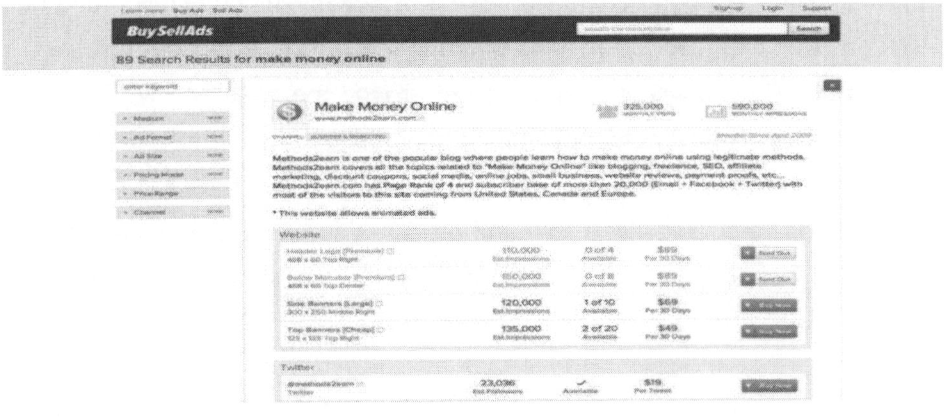

People buy these (as you can see by the fact that they are all sold out). In the case of this site (methods2earn.com), the site owner is making $2700 per month from his advertisements (when sold out), plus he sells sponsored tweets for $19 per tweet. He's probably making a cool $3,000 per month just for having those ads on the site, and that doesn't include the affiliate links and other ads he places inside of his posts.

The point of BuySellAds is not necessarily to copy other peoples' pricing. You should set pricing based on what you perceive the value of your space to be. You can play with it a bit too. Raise prices month to month until you reach a point that you don't quite sell out of space, then drop them back down half a notch. You want to sell that space for the highest rate you can while still ensuring that it all sells out.

3. Set Guidelines

It's easy to say anyone can post an ad on your site, but there are certain ads you'll never want to see there. I wouldn't want to post an ad for a product I panned in a review a few weeks ago or a site that has absolutely nothing to do with what I write about. Nor should you.

Set editorial guidelines for ads now and you can ensure they are easier to maintain later on when people start trying to circumvent those rules (and they will). In fact, this goes for all rules on your site - from comment guidelines to ad posting. People will always try to get around the rules and will inevitably make you feel like a jerk for not letting them do it.

So, write up clear guidelines now and be sure you post them before allowing anyone to buy ads (and follow them strictly!) Here are some examples:

158

* Content Type - What can the ad say, do or refer to on your site? If there are things you'd rather not promote, be specific in describing them.

* Layout of the Ad - How can the ad look? Will you allow text-only, images, video ads or all of the above on your site?

* Visual Content Limits - Can the ad only be certain colors? What about animations in the image?

* Ad Duration - Do you have maximum limits for any one ad or can someone book space indefinitely on your site?

* Landing Page Guidelines - What about the page that someone lands on when they click an ad? What do you allow and what don't you?

Ask yourself these questions before you allow anyone to buy ad space and you'll avoid having to remove an ad or change your policies in the future.

AdSense Strategies

You've probably been wondering why this chapter about monetizing your blog hasn't mentioned a thing about Google AdSense yet. The simplest and fastest way to monetize anything with a dotcom, AdSense is used on millions of blogs and other sites around the globe, so why not yours?

I have a love/hate relationship with AdSense, as you can see from my site.

Here's why. AdSense is an interesting animal, and if you really tweak it to its fullest potential, you can make a lot of money with it. But like any online tool, if you only do the bare minimum, it simply doesn't work that well. Google doesn't care that much since any clicks on those ads mean money in their pocket, but as a site owner and someone who strives to deliver only the highest quality content to my readers, I have a few problems with AdSense, at least in its out-of-the-box format.

As you read in the introduction to this book, I used AdSense to revitalize TechZone and jumpstart my income again through advertising. But, when someone asks me whether AdSense is a good fit for their blog, I usually say no – at least not right away.

AdSense shouldn't be included on any new blog because your goal at that point is not to have people click ads and leave the site but to continue reading your content and get hooked.

Essentially, with AdSense, the only way for you to make money is for people to leave your site entirely. That's not what you want to have happen. So, when your site is new, I say avoid it. But as your site ages, AdSense can be a powerful tool for monetization if you use it properly.

Adding AdSense to Your Blog

Placing AdSense on a blog is simple. Google makes it simple because more ads means more money for them and a greater market share. Very simple. But the problem is that it is too simple, and many people never stop to think about what the site should actually have on it. So if you have ever considered or are considering putting AdSense on your blog, read this next bit very carefully.

First, I use AdSense sparingly. This is where I place AdSense:

50 More Networking Passes To #ASW13 Up For Grabs

written by John Chow on November 1, 2012

Do you really want to go to Affiliate Summit West in Las Vegas but missed out on winning one of the ten Networking Plus Passes I had up for grabs? Well, all hope is not lost because Affiliate Summit is holding a sweepstake to give away 50 more passes! Go get it!

Entries for the Affiliate Summit Ticket Sweeps can be made by Facebook or Twitter.

There will be fifty Networking Plus passes to Affiliate Summit East 2012 given away, each valued at $549 per pass. Winners will be notified by email or

160

A slot in the post and it's a visual ad (no text blocks). Why? Because for my audience at least, those text blocks represent a lower quality site. People use those ads because they want to make a quick buck. They don't take the time to customize the ads to provide value to their readers and it shows.

Visual ads are usually matched better, especially with the extra work I put in to match the ads to my content and exclude unwanted ads. At the same time, they match the look and feel of the rest of my site.

Can you use text ads on your site? Yes, of course. But make sure they fit the feel and look of your site before you do.

Bid Gaps

When you place AdSense on your site, you are limited to 3 ad blocks and one ad link and search box on your site. That is all. So most people will max out the volume of ads shown on their site, but if you do this, you may be missing out on a big opportunity known as the Google Bid Gap.

The Google Bid Gap is the difference between the price and payout of any two Google ads. The more ads shown, the larger the bid gap, as the highest ads always pay the most and the lowest always pay the least.

Think of it this way – if you have three blocks of ads and the first block has all the highest paying options in it, you are not guaranteed to get any clicks there. After all, there are more of the low paying ads in those second and third blocks so you are watering down your ad blocks and making it more likely for someone to click something that has minimal value.

The key here is to balance the loss of clicks against the higher per click payout you receive. With less ads taking up real estate on your site, you will get less clicks – that just makes sense. But if the payout is significantly higher, the income may still be greater despite all that.

161

Of course, we have no way of knowing what the actual bid gaps are. Google isn't going to tell you this because, well who knows why, but they aren't going to tell you.

So to better understand what those bid gaps are, or at least which ad blocks perform best on your site, you need to monitor them closely.

To do this, create a custom channel for each ad block and watch them carefully to see which channel does best. If all three channels get 20 clicks per month but channel 1 makes $4 per click and channels two and three make less than $1, it may be time to cut down to a single ad block.

Section Targeting

The second thing that most AdSense users overlook is section targeting. If you haven't heard of it, that's because most advertisers haven't heard of it. For whatever reason, the vast majority of web users don't use the most powerful tools Google provides. For you at least this is about to change.

With a blog, you often get ads that are not really related to your niche. This happens a lot because the content might cover a variety of topics and you probably don't keyword optimize every page on your site – at least not to the level of an MFA site or a review site.

So, we need to do some extra work to ensure the ads that show up on your site are actually targeted to the content your readers need.

Google wants relevant ads to appear on your site and will reward you for the clicks you receive, so there are methods you can use to tell them what types of ads you want based on the content on your site.

Imagine you are writing a blog post about how to build a new computer. The ads for these types of keywords pay out very well with anywhere between $1 and $3 per click depending on what type of equipment is purchased.

However, if you also happen to tell a story about a peanut butter and jelly sandwich you dropped on your keyboard, you might see a few ads from Google talking about gourmet peanut butter or a local sandwich shop.

Those don't pay out as much.

So you can use the Ignore tag that Google provides to tell them that you don't in fact want ads on your site about gourmet peanut butter. Only the big paying ads for computer parts and manufacturers.

You can write about whatever you want, whenever you want on your blog and Google will still show the ads you actually want to have there – the ones that will pay out solid CPCs. This is so powerful that I cannot honestly believe more people aren't using it.

Competitive Ad Filters

The last thing I want to talk about is competitive ad filtering. Basically, you want to avoid showing ads for sites that are competing directly with yours.

There are a few reasons why this is important, even if you don't pay for traffic or sell products directly on your site. To start, there are plenty of advertisers who use arbitrage to make their money. This is not as effective today as it once was due to increased quality score guidelines and the restrictions Google places on MFA sites, but it still exists and you want to ensure it doesn't affect the payout you get from your ads.

Why allow someone to effectively steal your traffic for $0.01/click? That's exactly what the MFA and arbitrage based sites are doing, however.

On top of the fact that your AdSense income goes down, this probably pisses off your regular readers. No one likes being directed to a site that has almost no content and is filled with ads. Google will see this as a lost visitor and a low return rate – not good for your growing blog.

So to avoid this type of situation, you can use competitive ad filters. When you block those sites that offer you super low CPCs, you can increase the payout of the ads that appear on your site and improve the user friendliness of your ads.

Of course, since there is no "block low paying ads" button in AdSense, you'll need to keep track of the URLs that are taking advantage of the system and block them directly. To do this, use the AdSense Preview tool.

Click on the Link Properties to see where the link takes you. Do not click the link, however, as Google bans anyone who clicks their own links, even if you're simply trying to learn where the link takes you.

Of course, there are a few services that can speed up this process. For example, the Ads Black List will show you a list of 50 MFA sites that you can block, up to 200 if you become a paying member (Google only allows you to block out 200 sites with your filter).

It will take roughly 12 hours for Google to start blocking any of the ads you put in your competitive ad filter block. You can also add URL shortening services to your ad blocker as well, as these are often used as a bridge between AdSense and these super low quality arbitrage sites.

Does this solve all of your arbitrage problems? Not necessarily. But combined with careful management of the bid gap it will keep you from having any issues with your ads not paying out enough or leading to really cruddy sites.

When to Place Ads on Your Site
Ads shouldn't be put on your site on day one. This is a big problem I see with a lot of blogs, and it can be an obstacle to you actually making any money from your posts.

The first thing you should do when building out a blog is focus on content. Only content. Ads distract from this in two ways:

* They take away time that you could spend building content that adds value to your site.

* They show readers that you care more about making money than helping them.

In both cases, you are making a huge mistake by focusing on ads before you focus on the content that will one day empower those ads.

So, when do you make the switch and start placing ads on your content?

It depends on your site, its audience and the types of ads you want to place. I like to phase my monetization in over time.

Not only will you probably not get a lot of ads early on - simply because people don't know who you are and you have no page views to sell - but you don't want to plaster your site with AdSense. It's not effective with low traffic volume and too many modules look cheesy.

But you can start posting reviews and affiliate links early if you have a solid content base on which to build.

Why I Don't Use AdSense
Throughout this chapter I showed you how to set up and use Google AdSense for your blog, but you'll notice I don't use it on my blog at all.

I know a lot of you will want to use it, even if I tell you not to – that's fine, but I want to ensure you do it properly. Even following these strategies, however, there are specific reasons why I prefer not to use AdSense at all. They include:

1   **I Make More with My Own Ads** – By selling ads directly to customers using the OIO Publisher Direct network and WordPress plugin, I can sell ads directly through my blog. Forget sites like BuySellAds. This tool allows me to do everything I need directly. Selling ads is time consuming. This tool allows you to speed up the process and maximize your return. A great investment.

2   **Controlling What Appears** – Google doesn't give much control over what appears on your site. You can block 200 URLs – that's it. Want to block more? They haven't expanded that list yet.

3   **Bad Targeting** – Even with careful edits, targeting can often be well off base. Consider the kinds of ads that appear next to horrible stories. This is a horrible example of bad ad targeting. Admittedly, it is better than this now, but not by much:

4   You think Folgers got their money's worth by having their ad next to this news story?

166

Google uses algorithms and algorithms have glitches we can't comprehend. Then this happens.

SiteMatch Test

Have you ever seen a massive blog that charges an arm and a leg for advertising but has Google Ads on it? Check out this experiment I ran not long ago on ProBlogger:

Google SiteMatch allows you to target and show adds on specific sites at a much lower rate than direct buys. So I got ad space on ProBlogger for a pittance. The message is simple – don't run direct ads and AdSense on your blog at the same time.

And last but not least, and I've mentioned this before; people leave your site when they click on a Google Ad. It's the only way you make money so now you're forced to find ways to get the clicks without it hurting readership – that doesn't exist. You can't build a relationship if you chase them away with a CPC ad that pays you $1 or less.

Chapter Seven:
Hunting Down Loyal Readers

Growing a blog is not always easy. In fact, very few bloggers get lucky enough for a surge of traffic to suddenly just arrive on their site. You have to work for it and that means getting out there and building a loyal audience using every tool at your disposal - subscription services, your email list, social media and other blogs. In this section I want to talk about how each of these tools can boost your readership and, more importantly, keep those readers coming back over time.

Popularity is one thing, but you want your readers to be active - to post content on your site, to click on your ads, to ask you questions. That means they need to return again and again and occasionally forward a link to their friends.

There is no such thing as a standalone platform on the Internet in 2013. You need to build on every platform at your disposal and take advantage of every opening in your niche to build a readership that will support your blog and someday allow you to grow your site to the point of monetizing.

RSS Feeds

Have you ever wondered this symbol was for:

It's an RSS feed, and if you've never built a blog or subscribed to one before, you probably don't know exactly what that means. For everyone else, it is a familiar symbol that loosely translates to "save this blog".

A blog has a feed that software and websites can track and update whenever a new post appears. It's like a stock ticker or a newspaper subscription. It shows up every day whenever new posts are written.

So when someone subscribes to your RSS feed, they will get those posts delivered to their feed reader (or phone or tablet) every day when you post new content. It's a great way to drive repeat readership and it can be a powerful tool in maintaining connections with people who only stop by once every few weeks or months.

Boosting Subscribers

So, how do you get people to remember that button exists and click on it? Here are a few simple tips to get them on board:

*** Full Feed** - Some bloggers create RSS feeds that only show a small portion of a blog post in hopes that the content they post will drive traffic back to their site. Unfortunately, a lot of subscribers will simply ignore the feed if you do this. RSS is essentially ad free and people know it - don't try to cheat.

*** Hold Back Your RSS Count (for now)** - If you have a small number of RSS subscribers, don't share it with people. I consider this to be anything less than 50. Remember, people are like sheep - they don't want to be the first to do anything, especially to step outside their comfort zone. So don't let them know they are doing so until they can see that others already have.

* Broadcast the RSS Button - Put a big, visible RSS button on your site where everyone can see it. People need to know that it is exists and that it is what you want them to click. Of course, Facebook and Twitter are also okay (possibly better when you consider monetization options).

* Remind People to Subscribe - Don't forget to ask people to subscribe. Place links at the end of your posts, remind people they can get your posts on their computer any time through RSS and ask them to follow you as many ways as possible. A quick edit to the index.php file in Wordpress or a plugin installation can make this possible in every post (even when you forget).

Getting Subscribers to Visit Your Blog

Of course, there is a problem with all of this. An RSS feed doesn't contain your ads or your affiliate links (it can in some cases, but bear with me). It's a stripped down version of your blog and it lacks much of the branding that you integrate into your site, so it can reduce your total traffic numbers if everyone simply reads your posts in feed readers.

So how do you get people to click on the link in an RSS feed reader and return to your site and read the post there, where there are ads, videos and recommendations for other sites, not to mention comment forms? Here are some tips to do just this:

* Comment Baiting - Using FeedBurner I can tell people who subscribe to my site via RSS how many comments my site has received at any given time. If someone wants to contribute to the conversation, they can see that X other people already have. Remember how people are like sheep? This is where you can lure them into the pen.

* Video and Images - While most RSS feeds show some version of a video or image, usually smaller and thumbnailed, an embedded video or massive infographic often requires you to click through to the site to see it. At the same time, you can't just post a video. Every video blog post needs to be accompanied by a few sentences describing what they are about to watch. You need a hook.

* Old Post Links - Deep linking comes in handy here as people will see dozens of links in your posts pointing to older posts. When you click a link in RSS readers, it takes you to that site. No ad-free version of that.

* Slow Updates - Remind people that if they want to see your posts quickly, they need to follow them in real time, on the blog. An RSS feed only updates 2-3 times a day whereas the blog is updated constantly.

The ultimate goal of an RSS feed reader is to remind people of how cool your content is and then drive them to you site intermittently to improve your traffic and increase ad revenue. Use it wisely and that's just what it will do for you.

Social Media

Now that we've talked about the simplest way to drive readership back to your blog, let's look at the main method used more frequently today than in the past - social media.

This is the age of social media, and while there are probably plenty of people who subscribe to your feed and read it that way, a lot more people wait for updates on your Facebook Page or Twitter feed where they can read it on their phones, tablets, computers or (depending on what year you're reading this) some other high tech device that probably straps to the side of their head.

Tools like Facebook and Twitter are not necessary for a blog to be successful. They are, however, immensely powerful when used properly in conjunction with a blog, and they can both grow readership and help you maintain it.

First, let's look at what grows readership on a site like Facebook. Let's say you automatically post each of your blog posts to your Facebook Page where your followers can see it on their walls instantly each day. On any given day, someone can click that link, read your post and then click "Like" and share it with their several hundred friends.

Even if you only have 10 or 20 people following you on Facebook, each of them could have a reach of 100 or more people who have never seen your blog. That's 1,000 or 2,000 people potentially seeing any one of your blog posts, even with just 10 or 20 followers. The number grows rapidly from there as your Like count increases.

So, how do you use social media effectively to grow these numbers and how do you avoid getting stuck in that classic trap of too much Facebook and not enough blogging? Here are some strategies for each of what I consider to be the big three in social media.

Facebook

We're going to take a few short detours in this section because social media is most powerful when you use it in its entirety. This goes double for Facebook because, I'll be honest here, I hear way too often how Facebook isn't powerful enough for what people want it to do - namely, sell things.

But Facebook is not an advertising platform. In fact, it's even less of an ad platform than your blog (which is admittedly not built for marketing either). If you plan on using Facebook as a supplement to your blog to build your brand, I highly recommend that you spend some time better understanding what it is for and how it is meant to be used.

I'll paraphrase a bit from a book I read recently that kind of blew my mind (in a good way): Social media works when you stop thinking of it as an advertising platform. There is no outline, road map or blueprint for success with Facebook. Just talk to people, get to know them, build relationships and the trust will come with it.

Good stuff and spot on true.

The reason companies like Chevrolet are backing out of social media is because they don't get it. At the same time, the people who *do* get it don't really get it either. Just like the big companies that screw up their Facebook Pages, the agencies and social media gurus think it is a cure all for web marketing needs. Hint: it's not.

Facebook is a social network. It is designed to help people connect with other people. So when brands enter the fray, things get a little messy. You can be successful, but only if you think of yourself and your blog as a person, not as a brand trying to sell a product (your content) to the readers.

You have to overload people with valuable content, talk about all sorts of random stuff possibly unrelated to your blog, and whatever you do, don't try and convince people every day to go to your blog and read it, preferably clicking on something in the process. Social media works best when you step back from the precipice and use it as it is meant to be used, as a networking tool.

So how do you do this with Facebook, the world's largest social media platform?

Personally, I don't invest a lot of time into Facebook or the other networks listed below. When I do use them, I automate the process as much as possible and I take advantage of mobile technology to keep up with those I follow, to ensure everything is processed and uploaded on time, and to make sure all comments are replied to.

Here are a few things you should do when building out your Facebook Page.

Create a Page

Even if your blog will be branded with your name, create a Page to supplement your Profile. Profiles are for personal connections and friends and they are limited to 5,000 total friends. Pages have no such limits and allow you much greater freedom in contacting large volumes of people. Here's my Page:

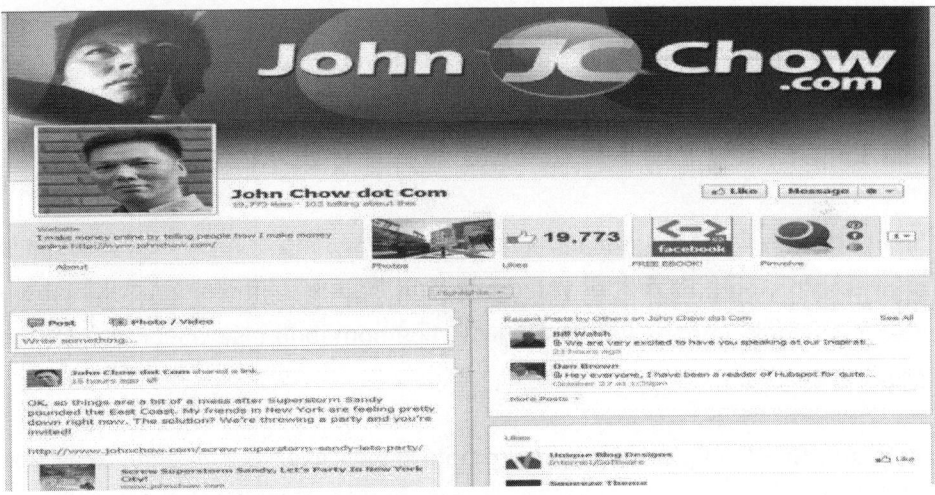

That's me and my nearly 20,000 likes. So, let's take a look at what I've done with my site:

1. **Blog Posts** - Share every post you write with a link on your timeline. Do more than just share the link though. Add a short blurb with it that people can see in their newsfeed and encourage comments, like this:

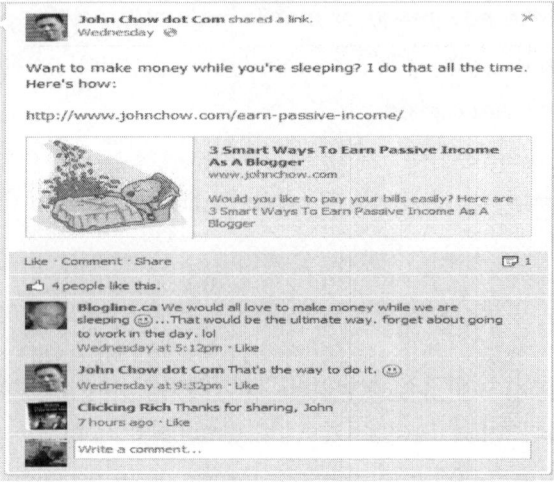

2. **Reply to Everything -** You won't find many comments on my Page that I haven't replied to. Get the Pages app for your phone (separate from the core Facebook app) and it will send notifications whenever someone posts something on your Page. You can then reply immediately from your phone and it will only take a minute.

3. **Share Fun Stuff -** If you find something interesting or fun that doesn't fit in a full length blog post or that you don't think fits the theme of your site, share it on Facebook. Images you find online, tips someone else posts or links are all good options.

4. **Promote** - Don't be afraid to promote things like your freebie. My Page has a link at the top to my free eBook. No one has complained about it being there. And I was able to drop the squeeze page code directly into Facebook as a custom app:

5. **Interact** - Set a quota each day or each week to reach out to some of the people who follow you and talk with them about their businesses, their needs and their readership. Look for questions they post and respond to them in a way that shows you are engaged with your likes.

Facebook

Facebook is an immensely powerful tool, but only when used properly and only when supplemented with real experience and authentic regard for your readers.

Twitter

Twitter follows the same rules as Facebook, but fortunately for you, Twitter is a whole lot simpler. If you haven't used Twitter before (which I find unlikely), here is the gist.

1. Create an account
2. Add people you want to follow
3. Write 140 character tweets about what you're doing
4. Talk to the people you follow

177

That's about it - Twitter is both a broadcast and interaction channel. Large businesses use it as a means to share information with people (something Facebook is not as good for), and smaller businesses use it to create relationships and maintain a public image of helpfulness. You can even drive direct clicks to your site through Twitter fairly easy (again, something Facebook stinks at).

If you look at my Twitter Feed, which has close to 100,000 followers, about half of my posts are direct responses to other people. I have a number of active conversations going with followers and people I follow (which is a very small number you will note). I also post all of my blog posts here, as I did on Facebook and I go out and try to find people to interact with at least once a day.

I don't spend a lot of time on Twitter - again, the mobile apps are immensely helpful with this - but I do make sure I have content on there every single day. Content is what I do and I know the value of consistency in producing it.

YouTube
YouTube is a strange site for a few reasons. I (along with plenty of other people) batch it together with social media, but it's not quite the same. In fact, when YouTube was created, it wasn't much of a social network at all. It was a repository for videos and people could leave simple comments. It was a lot more like a tumblog site (like tumblr or blogger).

Today, YouTube has been overhauled a fair number of times by Google to turn it into more of a social site, and that means many of the same rules of social interaction apply, but not all of them.

Think about how YouTube works.

＊You have a profile:

http://www.youtube.com/user/MotoTTZ

＊You upload content to a channel:

http://www.youtube.com/playlist?list=UUHHYPa7xpAukYw73GQ3jP3g&featur
e=plcp

＊You tag and distribute that content

＊People can subscribe or follow you and leave comments

So it's a content distribution platform with a social network baked in, meaning you could easily just focus on one of those two aspects and get it wrong. But you shouldn't do that. To be successful with YouTube, you must integrate the social and the content distribution and then you'll start getting a lot more views.

At the same time, you need to integrate the fact that YouTube exists with your other content. In my case, I generally just point people to my site where they can watch the videos. The content takes care of itself from there.

Connecting with Other Bloggers

The last thing I want to talk about in this chapter is probably the one that people neglect the most and ironically, the one that will have the largest and most permanent impact on your readership.

Networking

Networking is not just a fancy term for drinking with random strangers after work. It's a strategy being used by bloggers around the globe to meet other bloggers (both digitally and in real life) to grow their readership and increase visibility. When I say connect with other bloggers, I quite literally mean you should be actively making friends with and sharing ideas and thoughts with other bloggers either in your niche or in related niches.

One of the best things about blogging is that, while you can certainly have competitors, no one is necessarily a direct competitor. You should work with people, not against them.

A link to another site is an invitation for that person to check out your content and blog about it. I have done it plenty of times, and while I don't take many solicitations, I will often give someone a peek if I see them linking to my content repeatedly. It's only common courtesy.

So your job is to do some linking. Go out there and find bloggers you like, follow their content, link to it, post comments on it, ask them for feedback on your content and create a relationship with them that will ultimately allow you to reach a wider audience.

Think of the blogosphere as a big, unmanaged social network. You now need to go out and make some friends - it will be well worth your while.

Chapter Eight:
Optimizing for Google Rankings

I mentioned more than a few times in this book that it's not important what Google thinks of your website. However, if you want to maximize traffic to your website, it certainly doesn't hurt to be highly ranked for your target keywords.

So I want to spend a little time in this chapter talking about some of the strategies I used to improve my Google rankings, regardless of what Panda or Penguin do, and get high-quality, natural links to my website to boost traffic and improve my overall PageRank, among other things.

More than a handful of times I've heard people tell me that traditional SEO is dead. I disagree. I think it's simply been refined. Google likes the same things they always liked. They like high-quality content that is targeted to the needs of your visitors and that solicits back links from highly trusted websites.

The difference is that no longer can you cheat your way to getting those links. Before, there were dozens of shortcuts to find cheap and easy back links that would boost your rankings in Google quickly. Today however the simplest and most cost-effective way to really move your way up in the rankings is to simply write good content.

Since I've already given you my fair share of advice on how to write content that Google will see as good, let's take a closer look at a few other strategies - for things like how to generate natural links and drive comments to your site.

What About Panda and Penguin?

I love Google's naming conventions. No, seriously, it's a lot of fun. For years they've been slapping playful dessert names on their Android OS updates and now they are using quite possibly the cutest, least offensive animals they can dream up to describe algorithm adjustments that, frankly, make thousands of people irate.

Only Google would find a way to replace pictures of Gao Gao from the San Diego Zoo with cartoons of bloggers and Internet marketers tracking down a Google branded black and white bear.

But, beyond the amusement I get from Google's quirky practices, the truth is that I don't think much about Panda, or Penguin for that matter. They don't matter, and for me, they never have. Here's why.

I don't cheat.

I'm sorry to anyone reading this who got dinged hard by either of these updates, but the only way you honestly complain about this algorithm change without any hope of reversing whatever updates affected you worst is if you cheated, and in that case, I don't feel very bad for you.

There is no conspiracy by Google to encourage use of their PPC advertising platform over organic search. They are certainly using signals from Google+ a lot more than they should, but they aren't manipulating results by any means.

What Google is actually doing is trying to make their results better. A better product means more traffic, means more ad revenue - simple business model. We want the exact same thing, so whatever Google says is "better", we provide for them.

But more importantly, we agree with Google that the best way to build a website is to ask what the target audience needs and then build it. You shouldn't worry about what search terms have the least competition or how to rewrite something that got traffic for a competitor - you should instead focus on building your site from the ground up to be as successful as possible by providing value to your readers.

Then you won't care what Google's algo updates does, no matter how cute the names get.

Keyword Research

Despite all of that, keyword research is still an invaluable tool for anyone building a new blog. The key is to not use it as a foundational tool. Your site should still be based on people and not number crunching. But those numbers often reflect a lot of what your target audience wants and can be quite useful. Here's what I mean.

While I don't condone seeking out low competition keywords to ensure you get easy traffic, and I certainly don't condone using convoluted, misspelled or grammatically incorrect keywords (Google does not like this either, by the way), I do like the idea of learning more about what my audience is searching for and what terms they use to search for it. Here's what I mean:

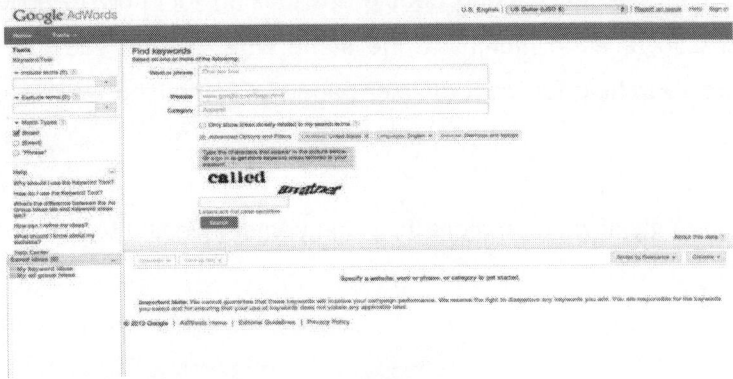

This is the Google AdWords Keyword Tool. It's built into Google AdWords, but is free to use, even if you don't have an AdWords account. Just go to this link:

http://adwords.google.com/select/KeywordToolExternal

You'll have to fill in the Captcha form with each search, but that's it. Now, once you've done that, let's say you are building a blog about building solar panels. Now, we could assume that the vast majority of people searching for this topic are interested in learning how to build the actual panel or we could do a Google search and see how many actual searches are being performed:

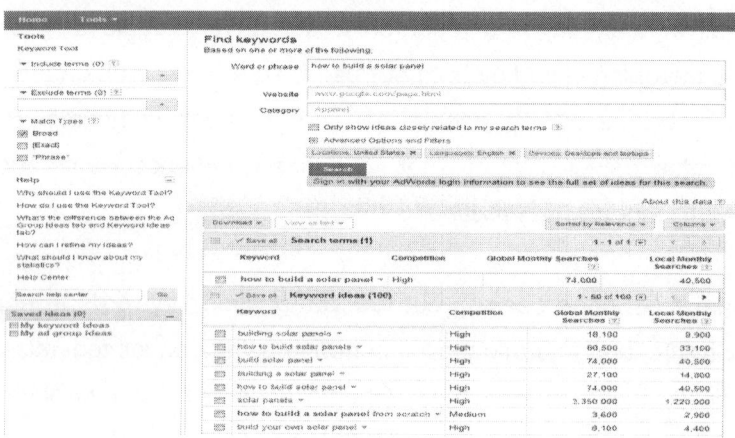

Now, we can see that 74,000 people are looking for "how to build a solar panel" in Google each month. At the same time we can see that 135,000 people are searching for "cost of solar panels" - something we may not have expected.

More importantly, if we do a more thorough search, we find this:

184

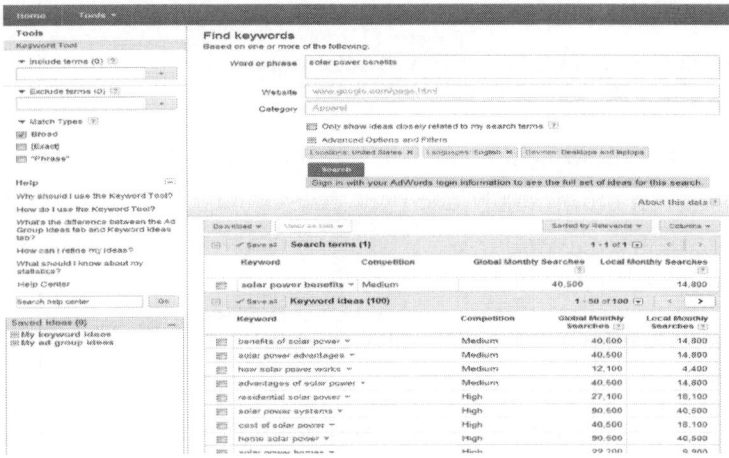

A LOT of people are looking for even more basic information about how solar energy actually works and a fair amount are looking for info about how to install prebuilt solar panels.

If we had simply started building a blog that focused only on strategies used to build solar panels from scratch, we would have an audience of about 74,000. But, if we built that same blog a little broader to cover topics like the science behind solar panels and installation and maintenance tips for existing PV panels, the audience grows by 150,000 or more.

That's a big difference.

Now, the same thing can be said for almost any niche. If you broaden it, you will almost always find more people who will read that content. At the same time, broadening any search will eventually water down your content so much that it will not have the same impact.

So when you perform a search like this, especially when starting a site for the first time, you should focus on a narrow topic that you can write at least 10-20 possible posts for and that will draw enough traffic. Don't try to be the biggest

185

blog on the Internet about solar energy. Be the biggest blog on the Internet about installation and maintenance of solar panels.

Then write about how solar works. Then write about building your own solar panels. You can grow rapidly once you have a handle on a core element of your demographic, but only then.

And keyword research makes this all a lot easier.

What does any of this have to do with search engine rankings?

Quite a bit as it turns out. Consider for a moment how Google would see a site that is filled with fifty or sixty articles all covering diverse topics on solar panel installation and maintenance. It would be a very useful resource and probably unique in a lot of ways. You may not rank above sites like HomeDepot or HowStuffWorks but you can certainly start to rank pretty well for target terms like "how to install an existing solar panel" or "how to keep your solar panels clean all year".

Now what if you were spread thinly across multiple topics related to solar panels? It would be immensely harder to rank for those terms because you would be trying to create authoritative content for dozens of topics all at once. Unless you are incredibly prolific, you wouldn't do very well.

Natural Linking

I want to move on from keyword research because, like I said, it's not as important as a lot of blog owners thing. A good blog is one that creates content that engages people and that naturally draws links and grows in the search rankings.

Heck, if you create a blog just right, you could quite literally only ever write new content for that site and you would be ranking for a variety of keywords in a few weeks. I kid you not.

So when it comes to SEO, one of our core strategies is natural linking, which amounts to basically assuming that because my content is so good and I have such a strong following, the traffic will eventually come my way. Sounds pretty simple, huh? That's because it is.

Natural links are any that come from someone who finds your content, likes it and places a link to it on their site.

You can of course encourage them to do so simply by creating content that is commonly shared. I'll go into more of what works for this type of content later, and again, check out the link baiting and viral content sections in the program, but what I really like to do is check out my competitors.

What are they writing about to draw traffic and how can I tap into that traffic?

Then, once you know what people like, do something bigger and better than any of them. Here's an example I point to from way back when my blog was pretty new still:

I saw that other blogs were blowing it up with articles and interviews with successful bloggers and Internet marketers. So, I went out and did some serious research and learned who the top 8 AdSense publishers were online.

The result was a post that has been linked to and shared thousands of times, drawing huge traffic to my site. At one point, I ranked number 1 for "whores" in Google. Algorithm updates have since knocked me down, but that blog post was a big success because I figured out what people wanted and then did it in such a way that was entirely unique.

Highly Effective Linking Strategies

Natural linking is great and will work incredibly well as your site grows and you start getting regular readers - especially if they actively share your content on sites like Facebook. However, there are other strategies you can use that work perfectly well with Google and that can help a brand new site grow quickly.
Before I get into what does work, I want to spend just a couple paragraphs telling you what NOT to do.

Seriously, this stuff does not work and even if it has not yet been pinged and red flagged by Google, it will be soon, because honestly, the goal of SEO is to show Google why your site is so good, not to lie to Google and try to convince them that your site is good when it's not (or appear that this is what you are doing).

So, avoid the following at all costs:

* **Profile Backlinking** - Profile backlinking is when you go to a high PR forum and create a profile on it, then hide an anchor text backlink in your profile.

188

This was very popular for a while because it tricked Google into crediting you with a high PR backlink from a forum with thousands of members. With very few exceptions, this does not work anymore.

* **Group Backlinking** - Where forums failed, group sites are now being used for the same thing. Essentially, you can create a group on a forum, social network or tumblog site and then create backlinks in that group that will point to your site, often with anchor text. Right now, it works. I guarantee it won't for long, though.

* **Link Wheels** - A link wheel was a very elaborate way to deep link your site without actually getting links on sites you don't own. I won't got into greater detail since this doesn't really work anymore, but the idea is that you create a lot of first level links on web 2.0 sites and article directories and then second level links from social bookmarking sites. Then you start linking all of those sites to each other - supposedly creating a surge of backlink juice for your site. Worked for a while but much less so now.

* **Bot-Based Anything** - If a backlinking method you want to use involves a bot or any type of software creating links automatically, it's almost certainly a bad idea. There are a lot of these out there like Xrume and SEONuke, but the idea is basically the same. Automatically create backlinks through a list of thousands of low quality sites. Google has caught on and it doesn't work very well any more.

* **Forum Linking** - Forum linking actually can work and still is very effective in a few circumstances, but I put it here for a couple of reasons. First, Google places way too much value on forums right now. Some searches will yield dozens of forum results, which are not authority pages since those people probably know as little as you do. Bing, on the other hand, gives forums very little credit. So I feel like the high PR days of forums are coming to an end.

That said, if you participate actively in a forum (15+ posts in a one year period), then you should 100% put your signature in your post as this can be very valuable.

Automated Blog Comments - Commenting on other blogs is a great way to drive traffic and get some link juice for your blog. I will talk about this more very soon, but don't use any automated tools to comment. Heck, don't even hire someone to do this for you unless you are sure they can provide high quality comments. Low quality comments, especially with anchor text in the "name field" are being dinged across the board right now.

Only Anchor Text Links - Google's Penguin update focused heavily on the habit many people have of creating links that contain almost all anchor text keywords. This is officially frowned upon now since it is technically a spam technique (hey, look at my keywords!) Use anchor text only where natural and make sure to mix in plenty of instances of your name, your blog name and your URL when linking back to your site.

Only Follow Links - This is the same. A natural linking profile will contain a ratio of follow/no-follow links between 60:40 and 80:20. So, if you have gone out of your way to get high quality links but 99% of them are "follow" links, Google sees that and interprets it as being unnatural. How much of an impact this has remains to be seen since usually it accompanies other things on this list, but you should mix in a fair share of "no-follow' links where possible too.

Paid Links - Paying for links used to work fairly well, but these days if Google suspects that a link is paid for (i.e. if it shows up on a "links" page or a "sponsors" page) they won't give you credit. It won't hurt you either, but it will not count towards your rankings, which means that, unless you are getting a huge surge of traffic from those links, you're wasting a fair amount of money.

* Link Swaps - Link swaps are similar in this regard. Now, a targeted link swap with a site in your niche and ensuring the links are in the content of a blog post and in context will be good for both of your sites. However, having a link swap section on your site or taking too many link swaps will only hurt you.

* Blog Networks - Blog networks are a good idea in principle. They combine large numbers of blogs into a network that shares content and ideas and helps people find what they are looking for. But like most good ideas on the Internet, it was eventually co-opted by people eager to get an edge in the search rankings and it now isn't nearly as effective as it once was. Public blog networks basically got hammered by the Penguin update, so you should avoid them at all costs.

* Low Quality Exact Match Domains - The most recent major overhaul in Google's algorithm was EMD or exact match domain. For a long time, people would go out and buy exact match domains like "sanantoniolawyer.com" and put the crappiest content they could on the site and reap the benefits of being ranked highly solely because of the exact match. If you've seen any of the "launch jacking" materials from Bring the Fresh or other products like it, you know the basic idea here. But Google is now dinging any sites that have low quality content on an exact match domain, even to the point of de-indexing those with really cruddy sites. Exact matches are still very valuable, but think of it as a piece of real estate - you wouldn't buy a lot on 5th Ave in Manhattan and put a Walmart on it, would you? You'd create a 5 star hotel or something like it - that's what you need to do with your exact match domain.

That's just a quick list but it should give you a good idea of what things I want you to avoid when you start promoting your site. Do some of them still work? Yes. I won't lie to you. A lot of these methods still work and there are intrepid marketers out there finding ways to make old strategies work again, but to be perfectly honest with you, I don't see the benefit in doing this.

Even if you do only things that Google can't punish you for now, they will eventually figure out what you're doing. Up until 9 months ago, blog networks were perfectly effective, but now tens of thousands of sites are down in the rankings - not good. Don't be one of those people.

Now, on to the stuff that DOES work.

Write Really Good Content

Here's the obvious statement of the day - write good quality content and people will visit your site. That may sound extremely obvious, but believe it or not, more than a small number of people focus so intently on the SEO aspects of their site and the links they receive that they forget to actually write decent content. If you want a site that will perform well in Google's index, you need a site that has so much quality content people cannot help but visit and check it out.

You need to drown Google in content, showering the Internet with stuff that it wants to know in your niche. My site has thousands of blog posts (over 1,000 in 2007, imagine what it is today). I write a lot and every single post I write is of the highest quality possible. I don't play games with content quality.

Visit Other Blogs

I go into this in more depth in other places in the book, but the idea is very simple. Introduce yourself to other blog owners, especially if you want them to link to your site. Right now, there might be hundreds of bloggers out there who would gladly leave a comment on your site or link back to your content, but they don't know who you are. There are over 100 million blogs online - if you don't take some time and show people that you know what you are doing

192

and that you are worth following and linking to (for the value of their own readers), what reason do they have to link to you?

Help Others and They Will Help You

I love helping other people out and I regularly link to other blogs on my site to show that. What this means is that I spend a large amount of time curating the blogs I like and putting together long lists of content that I think my readers would be interested in.

Just look at my site some time and see how many links I pump into each post. There are dozens, and while a lot of those are internal links to content on my own site, there are dozens more pointing out - showing people the kinds of content I like and what they can get from other sites.

Press Releases and Content Distribution

A press release is a powerful way to get attention to your site and it can increase your chances of getting indexed in a news aggregator like Yahoo! or Google (less likely, but still possible).

Of course, this is the easy way and costs you money. So the better way is to do it manually. Write up a list of blogs in your niche that would link to your site if your broke news on a topic they care about. My site curates a list of over 1,000 other blogs that are related to what I write about. When I have a big post that I want to share with people, I write a news release and send it out, encouraging them to link to that content.

Social Media

The simplest way to get people back to your site is to ensure it is indexed in social media content - on sites like Twitter, Facebook, Google+ (this is big because of Google's recent trend toward linking to their own content) and even LinkedIn if you have a professional-related topic.

I discuss social media at much greater length later in the book, but keep it in mind as a powerful strategy for generating links to your content and sharing those links with large, diverse groups of people online.

Link Bait 101

A little while back I talked about the whole idea of viral content and how it actually works - the fact that while you can certainly try to create viral content, not everyone responds the way you think they will.

This is the same, but it can be done a little smarter. Link bait follows the same basic rules as viral content. The goal here is to create content that other blog owners will actively link to. After all, everyone needs content, and if you create something totally awesome that they think would benefit their readers, why not link to it? (also, linking to other sites with useful information on them CAN help your SEO efforts).

So, your goal is to A) figure out what people will link to and then B) create it. Here's how I do it:

Step 1 - Gather Data

The easiest way to find out what people are linking to is to go on Facebook or Google+ (the latter being better because of its search function) and look for things with a lot of links.

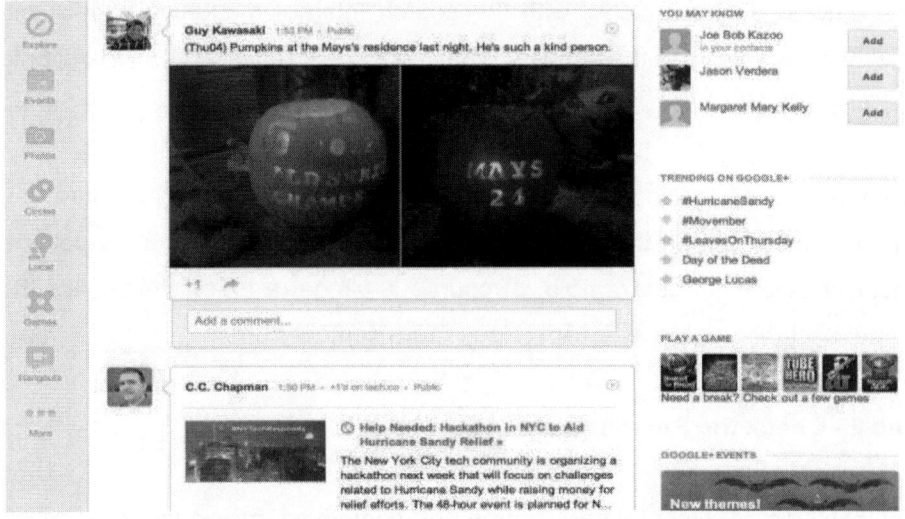

This is a search for Halloween. As you can see, the top results have a lot of +1's for that particular topic. That means they have been shared by a lot of Google+ users, a good marketplace for anyone who makes Internet marketing products.

The same is true on Facebook, though you'll find less of an Internet marketing oriented audience here:

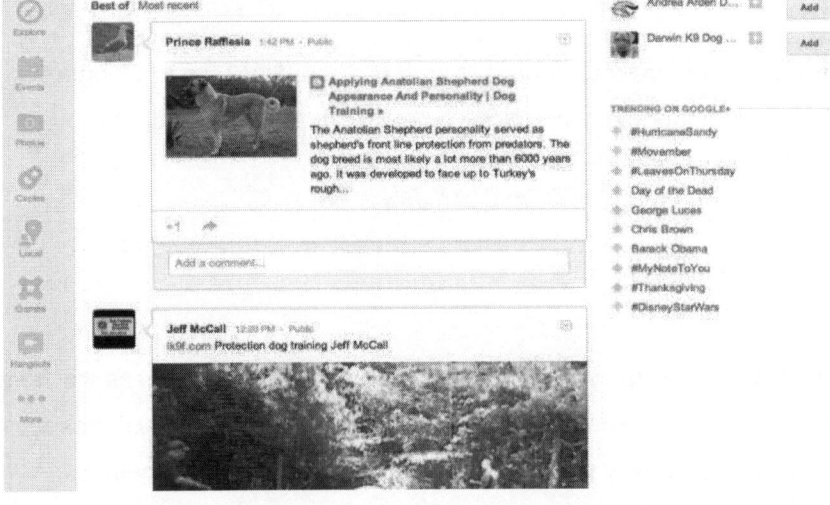

195

This is for a different niche, with the search Internet marketing. Check out how many people liked these posts. That's a lot of potential reach for a simple blog post or video.

Of course, when looking through social media for research, make sure you ignore any big names that you recognize. If you find a post from a political leader or celebrity, for example, of course it will get a lot of shares. It's the normal content creators we want to see more content from.

Step 2 - Check the Search Rankings

You can't go to Google and search for something based on how much feedback it has gotten, but there are a few shortcuts for this. Here are a couple strategies I like to use. First, make sure you are logged in to your Google account. Now search for something that you want to write about (or a topic in your niche in general).

Google will show you results that have names attached to them, especially if you have a lot of people in your circles on Google+. You can now see how often a piece of content has been shared right in the search results.

Method two uses a more roundabout search method. Here, go to Google Blog Search (http://blogs.google.com). Now, type in your search as I did here:

When the results pop up, you're going to see the most recent results from blogs that Google thinks match what you are looking for. Not all of these will have been linked to heavily yet, but the ones that have are good bets.

One last method that I like to use when researching topics is to go to the top site in my niche. In many regards, I am one of the top sites in my own niche, so let's pick a different niche. Here's one of the biggest blogs online - Mashable.com - it covers social media and technology news:

Now, every post on Mashable gets tens of thousands of page views and thousands of links and shares. But we can see which of the posts on Mashable perform better than others.

The above post has over 1,000 shares total.

This post has 1,050 total shares. Almost 800 more than the post below it. So, we know that this particular topic is very hot in this niche and will draw a lot of traffic.

I'm not saying we rewrite that page, but you can imagine the different strategies we could use to get topic ideas and generate new posts from them.

Step 3 - Create Sharing Opportunities

You can write the exact same piece of content in three different ways and get three different responses from your readers, including other sites that might link to that page. What I mean is that when you write content, there are ways to inject it with energy that will lead to people share it with their own readers. Here is an example from a post I wrote on my site recently:

It's short but relevant, showing a panel from a recent Superman comic in which Clark Kent quits his job to become a blogger. It was very relevant to my readers because it was about blogging and the changing of the guard from old media to new media. It was funny too. I made sure to fit in a few good links and a shot from the comic and it got shared quite a bit.

As you can see, I use a lot of different strategies to drive people to engage on that post and because I have linked to so many other posts within the text (a task few people do but that adds immense value to your posts), I have created a valuable piece of content that other people will want to link to.

198

Here is another example of a post that has gotten more backlinks than any other piece of content on my website:

This post got backlinks because it A) related to me personally as I am from Canada and know this area, and B) it was funny and interesting and I had something interesting to say about it. The result was more than 200,000 page views and reprints in major blogs like Engadget and TechCrunch.

I didn't do much different than I normally do, but it works all the same because I took note of what I thought would make a difference and integrated it into my website. In the end it worked quite well.

Step 4 - Trial and Error

You can only do so much research. Eventually you need to create content, and that's where you'll need to take a mild leap of faith. Eventually, when the time comes to write or record, you'll need to put your concerns aside and take that leap of faith that people will like what you write.

I can help you with this though - nine times out of ten, it won't work.

So don't worry about it. You have a free pass for AT LEAST the first 9 pieces of link-bait style content you want to create. Heck, if you get a surge of traffic on a post before you reach the 10th post, and we're not talking 10 total posts - we're talking 10 link-bait style posts - then I want to hear about it because you did damn good, friend.

You'll find that your audience is unique to your niche. Your personality, the content you write and the style you write in will all have a direct impact on the demographic of the people who end up visiting your site and reading what you write. That means that they will respond to your content differently than they might on another competitor site.

That's great, but it also means you need to do a lot of testing to see what people will actually want to read when they are on your site.

Take notes too. For every post, check your analytics after a few days to see what kinds of responses you got from the people on your site. Check for new backlinks, surges in traffic and comments, and any pingbacks you get on other sites. Don't necessarily change your editorial approach based solely on the backlinks you get, but be aware of what works and what doesn't and you can adjust if you're unhappy with traffic numbers.

Ideas for Link Bait Content

At the end of the day, there are a few types of content that work better for link-bait than others. This is not viral content, remember, so not all the same strategies we talked about in that section will work here. With viral content, you want people to share with other people. With link bait, you want site owners to share with their readers - it's a different audience.

So our goal needs to be to create something wholly unique that another site owner might not create. You can do this in one of a few different ways:

* **Breaking News** - If you can break news in your niche, you will get links. Not all bloggers follow the rules, but increasingly people attempt to source whoever broke the news on something first, which means massive surges of traffic to your site and untold backlinks.

* **Authority Content** - If you can create a piece of content that is so thorough and useful to the people in your niche that others can't help but link to it, you will see a surge in traffic and backlinks.

* **Resource List** - The same goes for a resource list. All those 101 lists are great because they take a lot of time to create and most people would rather link to them than recreate them from scratch.

* **Controversial Stance** - If you take a controversial stance on something with a well-reasoned argument, you can expect at least some other bloggers to point it out, either to argue with you or to make their own points. Don't be controversial for the sake of controversy, however.

* **Something Incredibly Cool** - This is a wide open one. You can write just about anything you want and someone will think it is cool, but can you create something that everyone thinks is cool universally?

Link bait is content that will add value to another blog without supplanting it or your own. Keep that in mind and you will create content that other people drool over and will gladly share with their own readers.

Targeted Link Baiting

Okay, so everything above will help you target...well, everyone. But what if you want to get links on specific blogs or build links immediately, not when people start seeing your content? Here are some targeted link baiting tactics I have used in the past to great success for my site and others like mine:

* **Write About Other Sites** - One of the easiest ways to bait someone into linking to your site is to write about their site. Go out and make a list of sites on which you'd like to see your links. They can be top blogs in your niche or even industry authority sites that you feel would be the ultimate backlinks. Now, write about those sites. They will see the links eventually and you can bet that it will get some attention, especially if you write about them repeatedly. This works in other situations as well. Write about your Facebook group for example, or specific people who Like you on Facebook or follow you on Twitter. Those people may now decide to link back to you because you mentioned them directly.

* **Interview People** - One of the easiest ways to convince someone to link back to you is to ask them for an interview. Interviews are incredibly useful on blogs because they bring in an outside perspective and they often integrate tons of multimedia - either in audio or video depending on how you conduct the interview. More importantly, 99 times out of 100 the person you interview will link to the interview on their site. Voila, you have a backlink from a trusted industry leader.

* **Take Pictures of People** - This works on Facebook, Twitter and your blog. If you meet up with people in real life, whether at a trade show or an industry event, or simply to have coffee and talk about your sites, take pictures. You can then post those pictures to your own site or social networking profile and

202

tell the other site owner about it - a lot of the time, they will then link to the photos, which happen to be on your profile or site. I did this to great effect after a CES event a few years ago - webmasters were lining up to link to pictures of themselves with the girls I had at my party.

* **Guest Posting** - I will be honest with you. I don't guest post on other blogs. I don't need to, and when I was building my sites, I didn't need to either. However, over the course of the last few years, after Panda and Penguin and Caffeine and EMD, guest posts have become one of the most successful forms of backlinking you can perform, even if it is a little tiring. The goal is to contact major blogs (with PR of 3 or higher) and ask them if they would like free content. You write them a blog post for free and they link back to your site. Google doesn't necessarily like it, but they can't do anything about it either as long as the content quality remains high, and in my opinion, if you want a guest post published, it had better be damn high quality.

* **Ask People** - It's easy to get caught up in all the intricacies of link baiting and forget that the simplest way to get anyone to link to your site is just to ask them. Ask for a review, ask for some feedback or just ask for a link. You can even ask for a swap between your site and theirs as long as the sites are comparable size. A lot of your emails may go ignored, but if you offer value to the people doing the reviewing, they will often at least consider your request.

This is just a short list of link baiting opportunities you can take advantage of. Don't feel like it is in any way limited to this. If you can think of a way to convince someone to post a link to your site, do it. It's well worth whatever effort you put out to get that link, especially today when the crappy, cheap links that you used to be competing with are so worthless.

Deep Linking

There are multiple types of links and each has a different value when it comes to the search engines indexing your site. So when someone links to your top level domain (yoursite.com) they are giving you a TLD backlink. When they link to a specific page on your site (yoursite.com/article-name-here) they are deep linking, and the perception to Google is that this is not only more natural, but more advantageous to the users of your site.

Search engines expect to see deep linking on blogs. After all, the majority of the value on your site comes from the individual posts you write. So, when the time comes to generate backlinks (or encourage people to link to your site) you should actively engage them to create links to the specific content you've created.

Now, the cool thing about deep linking is that you can deep link to your own posts fairly easily. So basically, whenever you write a blog post, take that opportunity to link to a handful of old posts on your site. Here is an example:

It sounds funny to me. The truth is, if your blog is hosted on a free server, you're not in control and anything can happen to your months/years of hard work. If you've $100, that's enough to register a domain name and get a web hosting service.

Bestselling authors always invest into their businesses. They don't rely on "luck" for overnight success. Investment is the only receipt, to cash out in the future. If you don't put in money, no matter how little, how can you expect to withdraw?

4. Work hard to earn passive income

There are thousands of ways to make money online. And you're free to choose whichever business model you want. But if you want to escape what *Robert Kiyosaki* calls, "The Rat Race," you must work hard and smart to earn passive income.

Passive income doesn't come directly from your hard work. Of course, at the onset, you'll have to work your butt off, but as time goes by, you can relax and still earn decently.

Writing a book can provide a source of passive income, especially from ongoing royalty. Also, Book fair and speaking engagement (where other speakers expand on your book and pay you for it).

Almost all of my blog posts look like this. They are filled with links to older posts that I have written that are directly (and sometimes indirectly) related to what I am talking about. In one post, I might link back to 10-15 of my older posts. They should, of course, be related to the topic you are discussing, but you can even get away with some offhanded random stuff if you make it clear that is what you are doing like my blast from the past style posts.

Now, this is less of a case now than it was years ago, but keep in mind that there are other blogs that will go through and curate, or in some cases simply scrape content from RSS feeds. Imagine how many backlinks you can get if someone steals one of your posts, linking to dozens of pages on your site with all those links in there. It might not be relevant and you might not always get credit, but a link is a link. On top of that, if there are links in your content, you can do a quick ping for trackbacks and see all of the people who are stealing your content (and then contact them about it).

On Anchor Text

Anchor text is a point of contention these days. For a long time, SEO's told you that your best bet was to create links only with anchor text that included keywords you want to rank for. However, recent updates like Penguin have tamped down on this a bit.

Anchor text is still useful, but like keywords in content, Google is slowly phasing them out of the algorithm as a major ranking factor. If they are natural, use them (this goes double when deep linking), but if they don't fit, don't force them. Keyword stuffing anchor text is risky these days.

AdWords Traffic

Last but not least there is paid traffic - namely through Google AdWords.

205

Anyone can pay for traffic on a per click basis, but you must ask yourself whether the cost is worth it. Paid traffic for some sites makes sense from day one. If you know you can make money from the traffic you generate, it will work over time.

However, with a blog, you need to reach a certain size first. A blog is meaningless if you don't have solid content and a large enough audience to enjoy it, and unless you have a few thousand in cash lying around, you can't buy that kind of audience.

But there are situations in which AdWords can make sense. For example, if you want to drive traffic to a squeeze page for your list or if you have a review for a high dollar value product that you know is converting well, paid traffic can ensure you get the kind of traffic needed to that post to boost the amount of money you eventually make from it.

Article Marketing for Traffic

One of the many strategies that we thought was lost after the Panda/Penguin one two punch in 2011-2012 was article marketing. Article marketing directories lost a lot of traffic and a lot of their rankings in Google because of the Panda updates, but the assumption that this meant they disapproved of the procedure was wrong.

While Google no doubt doesn't look happily on people who create articles with the express purpose of growing search rankings, there is absolutely NOTHING wrong with writing a valuable article that people will read and posting it on a high traffic site. It's a natural activity that promotes your site.

The key is quality. The articles you write for these directories need to actually be good.

Before I go any further, let's take a look at what article marketing actually entails.

There are a number of article directories online - sites that accept submissions of free content and then categorize them and publish them to the search listings. The business model is simple. You send them free content in exchange for a backlink to your website and they receive the ad revenue generated by your content.

In the past, these sites were often automated to some degree and had low editorial standards, which of course means that when Google integrated Panda and Penguin, they got dinged very hard. It turns out that Google does NOT like super low quality content being published solely for the purpose of generating back links. Go figure.
You're in luck though, because you're a content creator and content creators are Google's best friend.

The myth that article directories died in 2011 is seriously overblown. Here's what actually happened.

These sites were very large. Google's algorithm in the past saw that these sites had tens of thousands of pages of unique content and rewarded them accordingly. They had Page Ranks as high as 8 in some cases, and if you got an article published in them, you'd jump to the top for that page's keywords pretty quickly.

But, when the new algorithm updates entered the fray, they stripped away credit for thousands of $3 articles that people had published for the sole purpose of getting those links.

The directories lost thousands of pages in the indexes, and in the cases of those sites that didn't take editorial guidelines seriously, the sites were completely deindexed. Some sites were even shut down as a result.

But it's been a few months and the biggest of these sites have survived by making a few important changes. They now have strict guidelines, allow only original content and check it for quality. So no article spinners and no outsourcing to the Philippines for $3 per page. It doesn't work anymore.

What does work is writing high quality content and submitting it to the sites with the best standards. You can get some decent links and can generate quite a bit of direct traffic from these articles, especially early on when your site is new and you don't have a Page Rank of your own.

So how do you use these sites effectively? Here are some tips:

1. **Don't Republish** - Treat these sites like guest post opportunities. Don't rewrite anything from your blog and don't republish the content. Instead, only submit each article to one site (no multi-submissions) and always include a link at the end, but not necessarily with anchor text.

2. **Create Two Parters** - Don't put all of the content into a single article. The articles likely to get the most clicks are those with exceptionally high quality content that are short. So, keep the content on these sites short (less than 500 words) and then put a link at the end to the rest of the post on your site. Don't forget to link to the first part from your blog post too.

3. **Which Sites to Use** - There are dozens of these free article directories, but the gold list has shrunk quite a bit in recent years due to the quality issues they faced. EzineArticles is still considered among the best, while Articles Base and Easy Articles are okay as well as Buzzle. I also like using Web 2.0

sites like Hubspot and Squidoo. Avoid eHow and others like it due to the major penalties that are continuously being dealt out to any Demand Media sites.

The point of article marketing is to get a small boost of traffic to your sites and get a few good backlinks early on when your blog is new. As your site grows, you will likely shift the efforts you put into these articles towards guest posts that give you better results. More on this in a bit.

Guest Posting

I've mentioned guest posting a couple times in this book, but I want to spend a bit more time on exactly what it is and why it is such a successful strategy. To be perfectly honest, I've never guest posted on anyone else's blog before. It's not something I actively participate in because people tend to link to me freely without it being necessary.

But I do actively seek out interview opportunities and I accept guest posts on my blog (don't inundate me unless you have a killer post related to my topics), and I have seen the immensely positive impact such posts can have on traffic and SEO alike.

When it comes to guest posting, there are a few things to keep in mind. First, the goal is not strictly to get a backlink. Sure, this is a good way to get a backlink, but as I've shown you throughout the book, there are a lot of ways to get links to your site, and not all of them require you to spend countless hours contacting blogs in your niche and writing blog posts on spec.

So don't look at this solely as a linking opportunity. Think of it as a way to spread your name. When you get a guest post on someone's blog, they are essentially saying "I like this guy's stuff so much that I'm willing to let him write content for my blog". That's a huge branding opportunity, plus you get the backlink and whatever direct traffic is generated from that blog. You might even get additional backlinks from people referencing your article. It's a great way to get your name out there, and with social media, there is a good chance you'll get some serious exposure as a result of the content you write for guest posts.

So, how do you get a guest post on someone's blog? There are a few strategies.

Step 1 - Find Blogs to Contact

If you write a tech blog, you may not succeed in getting a guest post on a site like TechCrunch or Engadget when your own site is only a few days old, but at the same time, there is no reason to immediately assume you can't. So, create a list.

Start building a database of blogs in your niche on which you'd like to see your content. They can be partially related or a direct competitor for readers - remember, the blogosphere doesn't see competition as a problem. You all work together under ideal circumstances.

Step 2 - Create Content

Two things to keep in mind here. First, your blog should already be fleshed out to the point that it has plenty of content to view. If you want to post content on someone's blog, the first thing they will do is check your site and see what kind of things you are writing and what responses you are getting.

This is why I recommend using article directories at first - they don't check these things and they provide early backlinks. As your site grows, though, and has a month's worth of posts or so, you can start showing those posts to other bloggers and trying to get guest post opportunities.

Second, you need to have content ready to publish. Most blogs are big and have a multi-person editorial team. They don't have time or resources to work with you in developing a topic for a blog post. So write one in advance. Show them what you want to publish on their site. It makes it much easier for them to say yes (or no). Either way, you'll get an answer.

Step 3 - Follow Up

When you contact someone and don't hear back, don't assume it's a no. They get a lot of requests and sometimes they don't need content. Other times, they simply don't have time to reply to your message. Follow up after a reasonable amount of time (a week or two) and check in on the progress of your guest post. Often, a subtle reminder will do wonders. If you still don't hear anything for a while, feel free to write them and say you will have that content published on a different blog and thank you for consideration. Don't send an article to multiple sites because you risk having it published multiple times, breaking their rules and harming your credibility.

Step 4 - Meter Them Out

When you get a guest post published, you want to make a mention on your site, followup on any comments you receive on that site and thank the other blogger. So it can be overwhelming to manage five or six guest posts on a single day, or even in a single week. I recommend spreading out the requests you send over the course of weeks. Set a quota and send that many requests each week, ideally so that they don't bunch up if they start to get accepted.

How many requests you send will depend on how much time you have available to handle these things once a post goes live, and remember, you still need to manage your own site.

A Note on Sites

When you submit a guest post request, the goal is for the content you have published to match the content of your site as closely as possible. Sometimes you can stretch it, especially if there is a philosophical similarity or if the difference is strictly related to the format not the content, but you shouldn't be posting guest content for a tech blog on sites about dog training - unless the tech is related to dogs somehow.

The audience doesn't always translate and the link is not as valuable.

Chapter Nine:
What's Happening?

I've thrown a lot of information at you - so much so that you probably don't know where to start. Definitely check out the 30 day action plan when you're ready to start building your site, because it contains a lot of good information you'll want to use in the development process.

Before that, though, I have one more thing I want to talk about - something that can have a huge impact on your efforts.

Analysis.

I have a love/hate relationship with analysis, and for good reason. While part of me loves digging into the numbers and seeing where people find my content and how they interact with my site, another part of me gets a little frustrated when I see high bounce rates or low page reads, and frankly it can get very boring and a little overwhelming when trying to sift through all this data.

So to ensure you don't get a headache trying to figure out what numbers matter and which ones don't, here is a run through of what I do and how you should integrate the same strategies into your site's operation.

Google Analytics

Step one is to create a Google Analytics account and install the tracking plugin on your blog. I use Ultimate Google Analytics for this as it works well and is simple so it doesn't break every other time Wordpress pushes out an update.

Google Analytics is a powerful tool. You may not remember the days when data like this was incredibly costly - when you had to spend hundreds of dollars a month to see who was visiting your site and what they were doing before, during and after that visit. Today, website owners take it for granted, which is a shame because many of them fail to use that data to its fullest capacity.

While you can certainly overuse data (any data), Analytics is so powerful because it provides a simple, user-friendly front end and a super powerful, detail rich backend for those that want to dig around a little. We're going to be somewhere in the middle because, while I am all about data and using it wisely, there are certain things that should be avoided - most notably overanalyzing information that may not have as big of an impact as we expect on our efforts.

Statistics at a Glance

Before I show you the interface and how to find the information you need, let's take a closer look at a handful of metrics that I find important for my own site. These are measurements that Google takes of my site and shares in the Analytics interface, and a lot of the time, they can be quite surprising:

* **Unique Visitors** - The number of unique visitors is different from total page views. This is the number of people who visit your site each day, week or month (depending on how you view it). If the same person visits three times, they only count once.

* New vs. Repeat - You can see what percentage of page views for any single page on your site are from new visitors vs. repeat visitors. I like to see a high number of repeat visitors, but also a good percentage of new ones - 80/20 is a good ratio for most sites.

* Traffic Source - Where did your traffic come from? In most cases, this shows you how someone found your site. Until recently, you could see every keyword used to find your site. Due to privacy laws, Google does not share keywords used by people who are logged into their Google accounts - which is much more common now that Google+ has been integrated into their products. Still, you can get quite a bit of useful data this way.

* Bounce Rate - The bounce rate is the percentage of people who leave your site within 5 seconds of arriving. The lower the bounce rate, the more people are consuming content on your site well after they arrive. Google uses bounce rate as a measurement of SERP effectiveness. If you show up number one for a search term, but the people who click on that link bounce back to Google 80% of the time, they see that as your site not being what those people were looking for.

* Page Views - This measures how many total pages on your site each visitor clicks through. The higher the number, the better your site is doing at moving people to new content, which of course increases the odds of a conversion or sale.

* Conversion Rates - You need to define the goals before Analytics can measure conversion rates, but I highly recommend you do this. You can define a goal as someone clicking on an affiliate link or someone submitting an email address on a form. This will measure how many people land on a given page that converts based on your criteria.

215

* **Exit Paths** - Google will also tell you which pages people viewed last before exiting your site. This can be useful as you may have a page that is driving people off your site or there may be a link that is encouraging people to click and leave your site. In both cases, if your goal is for them to NOT leave, then you can make changes accordingly.

* **Time on Site** - Finally, you can see how long each visitor spends on your site. This is useful as a general metric, but also for specific pages, searches or entry paths to your site. See how long people stick around, and subsequently what pages they view while they are there.

This is a lot of information, I know, so before I go any further, let's take a few steps back and look at what you can actually do with this information. Because, as they say, information is only as powerful as the end result gained by using it.

Google Alerts and Social Media Monitoring

Google is a massive database that anyone can search to find content in almost any niche. So if you want to appear at the top of that database, you will likely put your name out there a lot. Unfortunately, this also means that you give other people opportunities to put your name out there and use it as they see fit.

Fortunately, there are ways to keep track of when you pop up in search results and in social media using one of several free tools.

The most powerful free tool available is of course from Google and allows you to set up alerts that will send you an email every time a keyword match is indexed. So you can set it to tell you whenever your name appears in Google, whenever your site name pops up or even whenever a keyword for which you

216

are competing appears in Google. These are all good opportunities to jump in the rankings by seeing what other people are doing and either do it better or do it first.

Google Alerts

Google Alerts is exactly what it sounds like. Enter a search term into the interface and Google will send you an email whenever something is indexed that matches that term:

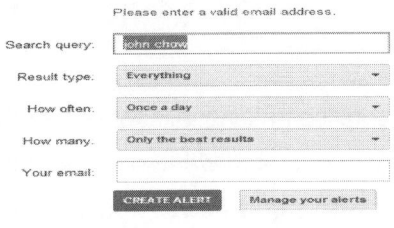
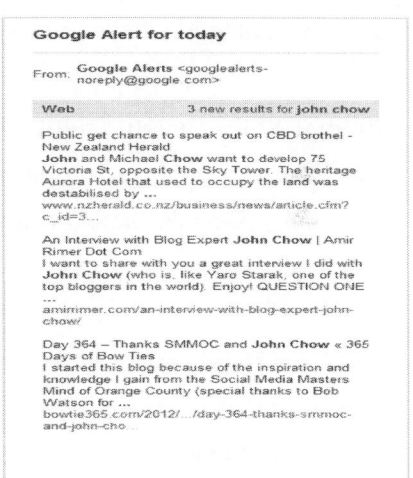

This is a Google Alert set up for my website name (johnchow dot com). If someone writes about me or my site, it will show up in Google's index eventually and I'll get an email.

This a great way to monitor your brand and respond quickly if someone says something about you that you don't like or that you would like to defend. However, it also has other uses. Here are some of my favorites:

* Track Competitors - Want to know what people in your niche are doing? Put their byline names into Google Alerts and you'll get an update whenever a

217

new post of theirs is indexed. Why Google Alerts and not an RSS feed? Because you never know when they will post a guest post or get interviewed by another blogger.

* Track Past Posts - You can track your own posts from the past to make sure no one is borrowing your titles or rewriting your content.

* Follow Emerging Trends - If a new product, service or brand is starting to trend, you can track it actively with Google Alerts to see what other thought leaders and bloggers have to say about it.

* Predict News Development - If you are sure something will happen in the news soon, like a merger or release of financial data and want to know about it fast, set a Google alert for keywords related to that news. You will hear about it quickly when it pops up.

* Look for New Products to Review - Set the names and brands of past products you've reviewed, as well as author or manufacturer names. It's hard to track all of the stuff you've reviewed before - either positively or negatively - so you want to know quickly when a new one pops up.

Any one of these can give you some great ideas for what to write about on your blog.

Social Media Tracking

While Google and other search engines can track some social media content, they aren't comprehensive and they don't track in real time, at least not the way a social search engine would.

So, to supplemental Google Alerts, you can also use tools like Twitter Analyzer, Tweeps, spy, or Twitterholic, among others. Facebook monitoring is

218

a little more complicated as many services charge for comprehensive coverage. But you can set up custom searches in Facebook directly or you can simply monitor the Insights you have access to in Facebook for your Page.

My favorite tool for this is Klout which I covered in a different section of this book, but if you want more powerful tools that allow you to see what people are actually saying and to visualize the data that is gathered, it will almost certainly cost you money every month - not necessarily worth it this early, but a definite possibility in the future as your site grows.

The 30 Day Plan

Day 1 - Outline Your Blog

Today's Goals:

The first step in creating a new site is to figure out exactly what that site will be about. What will you write about, what domain will you buy, what resources will you tap into to create your site? These are all very important questions.

On day one, you are going to sit down and create a detailed outline of what your blog will do, who it will target and how you expect to grow it after the first few days/weeks. This is not a throwaway activity. It is very important and will help you be ready for just about anything that might come up.

Why It's Important:

The biggest mistake you can make in the first week is skipping this day. Seriously, the background of your site is the foundation on which you will build it out. You need to know what you will present to people, how you will present it and ultimately, what you expect people to do when they visit your site.

Here are just a few things that a good blog outline will help you do:

• **Create the layout of the site** - How your site looks is very important as it determines what type of content you place there, where the ads go and generally how cool your site looks.

• **Choose which products to promote** - You can't promote a product until you determine who your audience is, what they would buy and what products you personally are willing to promote to them.

221

•   **Decide where to target comments** - A major component of this course is getting in touch with other bloggers and building a real relationship with them. So, you need to build a list of sites that are like what you want to create for yours so you can contact them in due time (we'll do this in a couple weeks).

•   **Generate strategies to monetize** - How are you going to convert all that traffic into cash (once you start getting traffic)? This is a big question so keep it at the forefront of your thoughts as you generate a site outline. You shouldn't monetize right away, but when you do, how will you do it?

•   **Create your content calendar** - Last but not least, you need a content calendar. I'll walk you through a much more in-depth process for this later, but right now start brainstorming what types of content you want to create and what problems you want to solve for your readers.

These are all very important things. The more you do with them now, the better you'll be prepared later when the time comes to grow your site, add more content or start reaching out to potential content or marketing partners.

To Do List:

Every day I'm going to include a list of action tasks you should complete that day. This is the stuff that you should be doing to ensure your site stays on track. Today's list is as follows:

•   **Who Is Your Audience?**
Step one is to ask yourself who exactly is going to be reading this blog. Ideally, who will find your blog, read it and post comments on it? These are the people you'll be writing for, and therefore are the people you should learn more about.

222

- ## **What Do You Like to Blog About?**

At the same time, you should ask yourself what you like to write about. A good blogger is one with a passion for what they do. What do you find most interesting about what you hope to write about? What got you interested in this topic to start and what keeps you interested in it over time?

Ask yourself these questions because if you don't have a good answer, you should probably pick another topic. The one with the most cash in the pot is not necessarily the best one.

- ## **What Do You Have Expertise In that Others Don't?**

I love this one because it so often gets overlooked (which makes my blog that much better in comparison). If you want to write about something, make sure you know your stuff.

Generic, filler content that you have no expertise in will get you nowhere. You need to know the stuff you're talking about, not only so you can talk about it like a professional, but so that you honestly have some interest (or per number 2, passion) in the topic).

- ## **How Often Do You Want to Post?**

How big is this blog going to be? This is important because you don't want to commit to posting daily and then get tired later and start posting every 2-4 days when you have time. Choose a timeframe you *know* for a fact you can keep up with and then keep up with it. Decide now how much time you can realistically commit to this project.

Day 2 - Building Your Brand

Today's Goals:

Some people would say that this should be later in the program. Others would say "to heck with it" entirely. But I think branding is much more important than all that. You need to know that when you start putting content out there it matches a central image you are trying to project.

That image might change over time. It might change rapidly at the start, but it should still exist and your efforts should always be built around trying to match it as much as possible.

Why It's Important:

Let's use a different word for a minute. Instead of branding, think of this as your story. Imagine going to a movie that you think is a comedy - a brilliant, highbrow comedy of manners. Then, halfway through the movie, the main character is bitten by a vampire and goes on a rampage, killing every other main character before melting into a puddle of talking orange goo that is licked up by a cat.

WTF?

You couldn't get more random if a ferret hopped on a unicycle and rode across during the credits (heck, let's say he did). The point is that you'd be pretty confused and probably a little annoyed. Almost certainly you wouldn't see another movie by that director.

It's bad, and more than a little unprofessional. Your brand is the same. If you don't take the time to control the image you project to your readers, you're risking inconsistencies that could ultimately derail whatever messages you've been able to convey to them to date.

So, today I want you to take some time and ask what image of yourself and your blog you want to convey to people and, more importantly, how you plan on doing so.

To Do List:

Another light day, but don't underestimate the value of doing this. There is such a thing as over planning, but spending two days determining who your audience is and how you will present yourself to them is not over planning; it is smart planning.

- **How Do You Want People to See You?**

Do you want people to see you as the ferret on the unicycle? Or would you rather they see you as an expert in your field? The key to building a good blog is to know what you want people to think of you when they see your blog and then to build the content around that projected image. Of course, you shouldn't change who you are or what you think to fit the needs of your audience, but you can and should think in advance about how what you say and what you do affects that image.

- **What Will You Enjoy Working On Most?**

There are many ways to run a blog, and many ways to write content for a blog. So, when the time comes to create a content calendar or to build a brand around the content you create, ask yourself first and foremost what you will actually enjoy working on. If you're not sure you're going to enjoy something, don't indiscriminately shelve it either. Sometimes, something may seem overwhelming or demanding of upfront but turn out to be a lot of fun in the long run.

- **What Experience Do You Bring?**

Make a list of your qualifications. You don't have to post a resume on your blog, but you should know that you have the qualifications needed to talk about a topic like an expert. You don't want to lie, so it's important that you recognize up front if you're lacking in knowledge on specific topics.

Does that mean you can't write about it? Of course not. If you don't know as much as someone else regarding a topic, just change the focus of your blog. For example, you could write about something from the perspective of a beginner. People love to read things as somebody works their way through it, often working right along with them. As your blog grows, you will become an expert in that topic and your site will have a unique perspective.

- **Identify Like Blogs and How Yours Will Compare**

Now it's time to go out and start looking for blogs that are like yours. You don't have a blog yet, so it's easy to find ones that match what you want yours to ideally look like. It doesn't even need to be in the same field. The goal here is to find blogs that match the style, tone and brand of what you're trying to create. You shouldn't necessarily emulate them, but you may see a lot of good ideas and how they're maintaining their brand over time.

Day 3 - Activate that Blog

Today's Goals:

It's time to get your blog online. Today we'll take care of a handful of technical tasks to ensure you have the right domain name, hosting company and installation for your blog. I cover all of these topics in greater depth throughout the main book, so if you'd like a detailed walkthrough make sure to check there (links are below for each section).

Why It's Important:

You need a blog online before you can build it, right? So, this is of course a very important step. I think the rest is self-evident.

To Do List:

- **Research Keywords**

Keyword research for a blog is minimal. You should never keyword stuff your blog posts, nor should you worry too much about the cost of keywords since you won't be paying for traffic (probably). But with that in mind, there are a few things to look for.

First, you can research keywords to determine what people are searching for. This allows you to better understand the difference between what you think is a good topic and what people actually want to read. Second, keyword research is very useful in finding a good domain name.

- **Choose a Domain Name**

Next you need a domain name. So, go to NameCheap.com and start looking for terms you found through your keyword research. Ideally you want a

227

keyword match for a dotcom domain name that has a good chunk of traffic. Google no longer rewards exact match domain names in terms of SERPs, but it can certainly help in branding your site and it's effective in helping people remember your site.

Don't be afraid to spend a few minutes searching the database for good matches to what you want your site to be. If you are writing from personal experience with advice, consider even using your name for this.

• **Choose a Hosting Plan**

I always recommend Host Gator to anyone who asks me which host is best. I use it myself and have never had a major problem. They are quick and efficient and they scale their services according to your needs. So, if you need a large volume of bandwidth covered but you don't think you'll get there for a while, you can start with a small account and build your way up.

- **Install Wordpress**

Finally, once you have a Host Gator account setup, now is the time to setup your Wordpress installation. This is actually a very quick and easy process, which you can go through here.

And voila, you have a site.

Day 4 - Technical Stuff

Today's Goals:

Yesterday you installed Wordpress on a new hosting account. Today, you need to make sure your new Wordpress installation is ready to handle all of the cool stuff you're going to do the next few weeks. This is where we install the plugins and tools needed and get the settings just right.

There are a number of technical tasks listed in this segment, so if you're unsure about anything, go back and check the content in the main book. I also have some more in-depth discussions on video and on my personal blog if you don't feel you quite understand. And of course, you can always drop me a message and myself or one of my staff will get back to you as soon as possible with advice for next steps.

Why It's Important:

All too often, once a blog is online and active, people decide it's time to skip ahead and immediately start generating content for it. But, since you're doing this in one streamlined process, you might as well take the time needed to get it right. Install the necessary tools on your blog, build out your site properly and be ready to do whatever it takes to get as much traffic and readership as possible. That's what today all is about.

To Do List:

• **Set Basic Wordpress Settings**
In WordPress, make sure to set the following thing.

1. **Permalinks** - Permalinks are very important for SEO and must be set immediately. Do this now and set them to "%category%/%postname%/

2. **Theme Settings** - Install your theme of choice and review all settings in the theme's menus. Do this right away to avoid any issues later on. You can always post questions now to the forums for that theme as well and get it fixed early.

3. **Graphics** - If you need graphics, get them now so your site looks finished - you can always upgrade later, but the last thing you want is for your site to look unfinished.

There are number of other settings, many of which I covered in the book, so if you have the time Orage students heading all of them, you can do so as well.

• **Install Plugins**
Install these plugins for your blog:

http://bloggingwithjohnchow.com/membersarea/module-2-launching-your-blog/plugins/

Make sure the settings are established for all of them before continuing.

• **Familiarize Yourself with the Wordpress Dashboard**
Spend some time reviewing the Wordpress Dashboard and getting to know where everything is.

• **Set Sidebars and Widgets**
Set the sidebars and widgets for your site. Many themes allow you to have multiple sidebars so decide if that is something you would like to do now. Then go to the Widgets menu and choose what you would like to appear.

231

Don't let your sidebar get too crowded and remember you can always change it in the future. But ensure you fill that white space as soon as possible.

Day 5 - Writing from the Start

Today's Goals:

Okay guys, today is the big day. Today it is time to start writing content for your blog. It's been a few days and you've done your fair share of technical tasks and the result is your own blog, ready to use and probably already getting indexed by Google. But for it to take off, you of course need a good chunk of content for it. Today you will start writing, recording and brainstorming for future content.

Why It's Important:

A blog is nothing without content. I don't care how pretty your theme is or how much work you put into getting the theme and plugin settings just right - no content means no blog.

So, today I want you to write something, anything really. It's time to start generating content to fill the gaps on that blog and ensure it is ready for the flood of traffic you're about to get.

To Do List:

• **Brainstorm a List of 10-20 Topics**

Before you write anything, sit down and brainstorm a list of as many topics as you can think of. Even a small list of just 5-10 topics is good, but more is always better. Why so many? Because the more you can think of, the better chance you'll land on a select few that you really want to write about.

It also helps you create a longer list for later when you start creating your content calendar. Don't feel like you need to write about all of these. Some ideas will be boring, others redundant and others still just not very good.

- **Write 1-2 Posts**

Now it's time to start writing. Choose one or two of your favorites from the list you just generated and start writing them. It's been a few days now and you need to get some content online, so even if you get nothing else done today, make sure you finish one good post that you can post to your blog.

- **Experiment with Video or Audio**

Don't be afraid, even on day one, to experiment with audio or video for your blog posts. Video blogs are surprisingly fun to create and audio is a great way to start building toward a podcast or simply to brainstorm and start thinking of some good ideas for your site.

- **Edit and Upload 1 Post with an Image**

You need at least one blog post done today, but if you get more than one done, apply this step to all posts. Edit that post, then upload it to your blog with at least one image for every 500 words of text.

Try to keep your posts short to start. Don't write anything extensive or very long yet as you want to ensure you get a feel for what you enjoy writing and what people like to read. Plus, those first few posts will get smaller readership, so save your big long posts for later when you have more people to show them to.

- **Submit Your First Blog Post to Facebook and Twitter if You Have Them**

If you have Facebook, Twitter, Google+ or other social media accounts, start posting your content there. You can automate this process with services like NetworkedBlogs or you can do it manually. Plugins for Wordpress are available for Facebook and Twitter as well to automate posting of certain kinds of content. So, if you want to speed the process up, you can install one of those.

Day 6 - Choosing a Theme

Today's Goals:

I skipped this the other day because, to me it never quite works to choose a theme until you have a few good pieces of content on your site. So today I want you to write a few more pages of content (try to get to 4-5 total to fill in the front page) and then we are going to look for a new theme that will capture what you are trying to do.

Why It's Important:

A good theme will capture everything you outlined on days 1 and 2 - the brand of your blog, your personality and the type of content you are producing. People may not see the theme first and foremost but it can have an impact (either positive or negative) on your site as a whole so I take this step very seriously.

To Do List:

- **Write More Content (up to 4-5 posts)**

How much content you write will depend on your site and what your plans are for the content. On day 8 we will talk about content calendars, so for now just write as many posts as you have time to write - I say 4-5 but if you can only another 1-2 then do that many. How fast you write and what types of ideas you have will probably impact how often you post content on your site and what level of detail is included in those posts.

Some people feel comfortable writing posts every single day (or more often) while others only have enough time to post once every week or so. Regardless of which option you select, you need to stick to it because people will get used to that schedule. So pay close attention to your speed now and stick with it.

- **Research Themes for Your Site**

Take a look at the resources provided in the book and decide whether you want a paid or free theme and then which theme you would like.

Free themes you can install as many of as you want and just test to see how they look. Paid themes are less flexible, though with some theme directories, like Woo Themes or Elegant Themes, you get access to all their content with a membership plan, so you can test a dozen or more themes at once to see which you like better.

- **Choose and Install a Theme**

Once you choose a theme, it's time to install it. Learn more about how to do this on:

http://bloggingwithjohnchow.com/membersarea/module-2-launching-your-blog/themes/

Under appearance, choose themes and then upload. Upload the theme in a zip folder that was supplied by wherever you downloaded it from. Then it will be installed and you can select it for use.

This will allow you to use the theme immediately, though some themes require further customization before they can be used, so you may want to read the documentation for that theme first.

- **Customize and Finalize Your Theme**

After reading documentation, finalize your theme and its settings and then make sure it is ready to use. Every theme has a number of settings that are unique to that theme. So, make sure you check all of them, understand exactly how to alter what your theme looks like and then make a list of anything you need to add later.

• **Order Graphics for Your Theme**

If you purchase a custom theme and want to add graphics to it, I recommend you order them as early as possible. Don't spend a fortune on the graphics for your blog, especially since you haven't finalized how it's going to look and feel. However, make sure that you have something up there so it looks as you imagine it should. You want to start matching that brand as soon as possible, so you can start building out the site for future upgrades.

Day 7 - Claim Your Territory

Today's Goals:

One of the most important things you can do once you've written a blog post is to share it with people through as many mediums as possible. But you need to have accounts on those mediums to do so.

Today we are going to claim our territory on major social media sites, web 2.0 sites, other blogging platforms and anything else you can think of that will help you promote your blog and grow your network of possible distribution options.

Why It's Important:

This is immensely important. More than ever before, a blog can be successful if you find ways to tell people that you're writing it. If you can't do that, then you might as well write in a journal at night because you'll have roughly the same readership. I like to ensure my readers can be reached in as many ways as possible because not everyone uses the Internet in the same ways.

That's what this does.

To Do List:

• **Check Your Name or Brand in Knowem.com**

This is an awesome site. Basically, it allows you to check any brand or name across dozens of different social media and social bookmarking sites to see if it is available. Just punch in the name and it will run it through and check. If it is not available, you may want to consider slight tweaks to ensure you get as many available options as possible. Of course, you can always have different

239

names and different services, but it's not as effective when it comes to branding. I recommend you have the same name across every service.

- **Register Every Site You Can**

When you find a name that really fits your brand and personality, register it across every site you can. Use the list on knowem.com to build out that registration portfolio. Are you going to use all of these right away? Probably not. However, it's good to have them now instead of worrying later about how to get a name that matches your brand.

- **Create a Notebook or Evernote Folder with Logins**

However you like to keep track of things, create a new file or open a new page in your notebook and write down the logins for all the sites you just created. You may think you'll remember all of them, but trust me you won't. It's also a good idea to not use the same password for everything, especially if you're planning on growing your brand through the site. The last thing you want is someone hijacking all of your sites and broadcasting things you would never say.

- **Setup Facebook Pages and Twitter Feeds for Your Brand.**

If you haven't done so yet, create a Facebook page and a Twitter feed for your brand. Make sure that both are populated with all the necessary information, have a nice face headshot of you or your brand logo, and any other information you want people to know.

You don't need to start adding content feeds yet, we will do that later, but you should ensure that it is ready to use as soon as you have content to add.

- **Submit Your Last Two Blog Posts to Each Feed**

Whatever blog posts you've written already, upload them to both Facebook and Twitter. You probably don't have much readership yet, but you can start broadcasting your posts now as you start to grow your brand.

Day 8 - Content Calendar Creation

Today's Goals:

One week in. Take a moment, look back and see what you've been able to accomplish. You have at least 5 blog posts already, a killer new theme, a clear idea of your brand identity and who your audience is, as well as how you will reach them. There is a lot of good information in your head and now it's time to get it all ironed out and plotted so you can start sharing it with the people who matter most - your readers.

Why It's Important:

A good content calendar does a few things. First, it ensures you have enough ideas that you don't get bogged down by writer's block at any point. Second, it makes it easier to get ahead of the curve, having blog posts ready to publish before publication date. This is vital so that a small hiccup in your schedule doesn't completely derail all the hard work you've done.

A good blog is like a consecutive starts streak in baseball. You can start 2,632 times in your career but if there were 2,633 games and you missed one, you won't beat the streak. Your blog is only as powerful as the consistency you put into it. So, make sure you are ready at all times. A content calendar makes this much easier to do.

To Do List:

• **Brainstorm a List of 20 Topics**
It's early, but I like to have a huge list of content topics in front of me at all times. So sit down and write up 20 topics about whatever you can think about in your niche. They can be directly related to what you want to write about or

242

they can be completely unrelated topics, but make sure you have at least 20 of them.

•   Check Competitor Sites

If you're running out of ideas at any point or if you simply don't know where to start, go to a blog (or multiple blogs) in your niche and look at what your competitors are writing about. Don't steal anything, but don't be afraid to jot down quick ideas for what you can build on. You'll be surprised by how many options are here to grow out your site. Heck, you might even come up with some really killer topics that don't match your original outlines.

•   Create a Spreadsheet

In Excel or Numbers, or if you have neither you can use Google Drive, create a quick spreadsheet. Jot down all the content topics you brainstormed in step one and step two in the spreadsheet.

This will be where you keep all of your topic ideas. I like Google Drive, simply because I can add to it from anywhere, and I can share with people if someone wants to contribute a guest post.

•   Make a List of Content Types You Want to Make

Right now all you have is rough topics. Now, ask yourself how you want to present that information. Remember, you don't have to write everything you think of. Especially if you're not a prolific writer, you may want to do a lot of videos. Maybe you would prefer to make infographics or a podcast - whatever you decide you want to make, make a list now and start matching them to the content topics developed in step one.

•   Generate Hooks for Your Content

You don't have to do this for everything on your list, but you should start doing it with the ones you like the most. The goal here is to make sure that when you are writing any of them you have enough information in your head or written down to get going.

Here's why I do this.

Imagine you have a genius idea - one that you think could really go viral, so you write down the title of that topic and come back to it two weeks later to work on.

But you have no idea what you were thinking when you wrote that title down - what the heck is a "content storm"?

Whenever you add something to your content calendar, write a short hook or description of what it will be about. This can be the first paragraph of the blog post, a short synopsis of what you want to cover in that blog post, or even just a joke or hook that you can use to build from. The goal is to ensure you remember exactly what your great idea was so the writing goes more smoothly.

- **Start Writing**

Now start writing. You will probably notice that throughout this 30 day action plan I don't often tell you to write a blog post. Instead, every day I have you working on something new. That's because you should always be writing. Everybody has a different schedule and a different style of writing that works for them. So, if it works for you to sit down and write 10 blog posts in one day, do it. If you prefer to write one every day for the next week, do that. Blogging is flexible - as long as you are consistent and post on schedule, it works.

Just make sure you start writing. I'm not to remind you every day to do it. Instead, you should enter it into your calendar or to do list and take care of it whenever works best for your schedule each day.

Day 9 - Create Your List

Today's Goals:

A hugely powerful tool for any website, blog or not, is the email list. A good email list allows you to reach out to your prospects whenever they are online, wherever they are. They don't need to visit your blog - you can hit them up on their phones or laptops directly. But they need to opt in first and that means you need to convince them to opt in. So, today we are going to work on creating a plan for how to do that.

Why It's Important:

I can't stress how important (and profitable) it is to have a good list in place for your blog. The benefits you will gain by having a good list in place is immense. We're talking about better return visitor numbers, more traffic to your website in general, and much higher conversion rates for products you promote on your blog (or ones you create yourself).

It's not quick, nor is it necessarily simple to build such a list but the payoff is so great that I strongly encourage you to do it today and to followup on it daily, making it part of your regular routine.

To Do List:

- **Design and Start Building a Freebie**

As you build your list, think about what you're going to give away for free to get people on it. There are a lot of options here. I cover most of them in the book, including free courses made of emails or videos, free e-books, free services such as the Wordpress installation I offer my visitors, and pretty much anything else you can think of that's free. Decide right now what you want to give away, and start developing that product.

- **Signup for an Autoresponder and Create a Form**

The next step is to sign up for the autoresponder you want to use for your site and create a form. For my site I use Aweber.

The sign-up process takes about five minutes, and usually for the first month it's either free or costs only one dollar. After the first month it will cost between $15 and $20. However, I can guarantee that it's well worth the money spent.

I won't include a full walkthrough on setting up your autoresponder here, especially since most of these sites will walk you through it. So, before going on, follow the walkthrough in Aweber or whatever other service you choose and create a form for your site.

- **Install Opt-in Forms on Your Blog**

One of the cool things about WordPress is that you can use a plug-in for any of the major autoresponder services to add a form automatically to your website. I have a built-in widget on the side of my blog as you can see below as well as a pop over for people to sign up. You can install both or only one of them depending on how you want people to see your often offer when they visit your site.

Another option is to create a squeeze page and drive traffic there to sign up for your free offer. I cover this in a lot more detail here.

- **Create the First Three Autoresponders**

When you create a list, make sure you have a solid stable of emails to send out once that list starts to grow.

Autoresponders by definition are emails that are sent automatically after a certain number of days. Since this number is different for each person

246

depending on when they sign up, you should create content before you launch the opt-in form.

Today, create three autoresponders. Tomorrow and beyond you will work on more of these to ensure you have a solid volume of content in place before anyone signs up.

Day 10 - Content for Your List

Today's Goals:

The reason a list is so much work is that it is an entirely new outlet for content. You need a lot of extra content for your list to be successful, and it can't just be a rehash of the content already on your blog. You need more content, better content, more unique content that will hold and lure people back to your site or to buy a product you are selling or promoting.

Today, we are going to work on creating the content needed to make this happen and to ensure that your site has everything necessary to support and encourage the signup of people to that list.

Why It's Important:

Again, list building is super important. We're talking about a one way access path to people's most personal content library - their email. Toss in a heavy dose of trust and you have a surefire recipe for much higher conversion rates and more profits from the same volume of readers.

So, having a good content base for your list is a must. That's our goal today.

To Do List:

• **Outline and Start Writing 10 Autoresponders**
Yesterday you created your list and wrote the first three autoresponders. today I want you to continue writing. Remember that auto responders are generally a little shorter than blog posts, usually between 250 and 400 words. Additionally, they are informal and don't need to be highly produced with images or videos. It's just text, often with some links back to your website. A

good autoresponder is like a conversation, often telling a story over the course of many emails. At first it might take some time to get the hang of it, but by the time you reach thirteen of them, they should flow quickly.

Keep in mind that you can send them slightly less often if you supplement with broadcasts that include links to your new blog posts. I don't recommend you do this for every blog post unless you only post once a week. However, you can send out a weekly update that includes an outline of all the posts you've written during the week along with any news related to your site.

- **Finish Your Freebie (or work on it)**

If you haven't yet, finish writing or developing the free offer you're going to give away to get people on your list. If it's an eBook or something significantly longer than a normal email or blog posts, you may want to spend the next few days working on it. However, don't launch your opt-in form until the freebie is ready.

- **Add List Broadcasts to Your Content Calendar**

If you want to send broadcasts along with your scheduled auto responders, add it to your content calendar so you don't forget. A good recommendation is to send an email out once a week highlighting any blog posts or news on your site for that week.

You can also send broadcasts for new product launches, discussion of a review you've written on your blog, or to announce something in your personal life. If it's not spontaneous, however, add it to your content calendar so you can meter out when you write these.

Day 11 - Fill in the Pages

Today's Goals:

Your blog is not just an online journal. With time it will become a hub for information in your niche. So it needs to be easy to use and have enough resources that if someone has a question or needs to find something, they can do it right from your site. No need for them to go back to Google or to contact you or get frustrated.

Posts will only get you so far in this regard. So, today I want to talk about different pages you may want to add to your site. Most blogs don't need many of these, but depending on what you are promoting and writing about, there are a few you should consider.

Why It's Important:

Usability is a key metric measured by Google on websites when determining SERPs. If your readers leave the site quickly or if they click around too much not finding what they need, Google can tell and you can be penalized for that. So, it is in your best interest to create an easy to use site.

Not only that, but an easy to use site is one that your visitors will stay on longer and use more frequently. Good, powerful, and well-built websites are the lifeblood of an online business. It's more professional when it's quick and easy to use and it's more effective when you try to convert people to whatever products you are promoting.

To Do List:

• **Draw an Outline of Your Site's Navigation**

One of the easiest ways to ensure you don't miss a page, and to speed up the process of developing your site's navigational structure, is to draw an outline. Sit down and draw on a piece of paper how you want your site to operate.

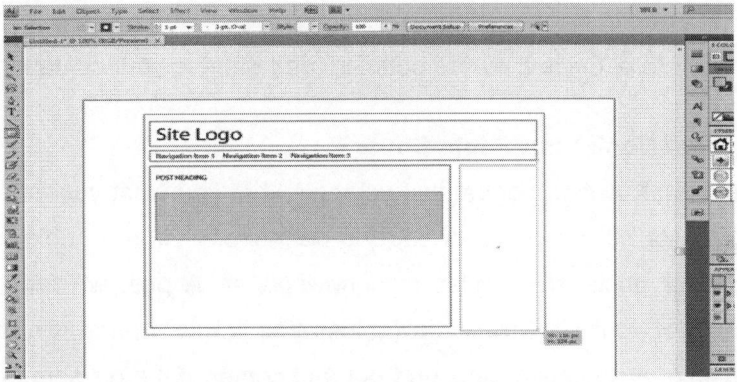

This is a wireframe. It's basically a drawing of exactly how the website will look when it's up and running. Since your website is already up and running, I recommend you do something slightly more than this.

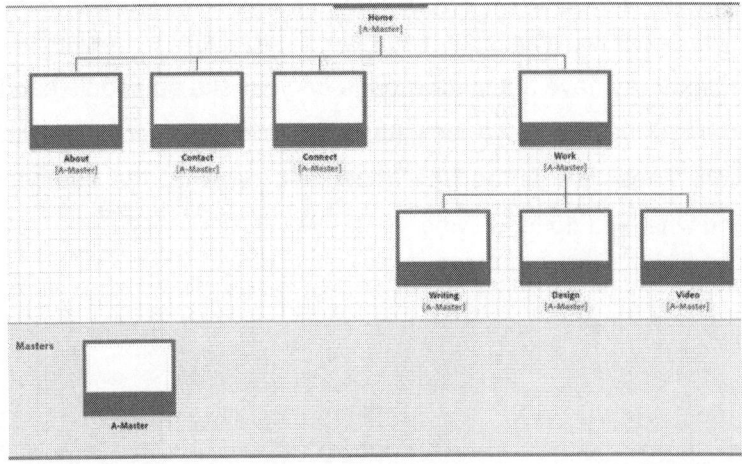

This is a navigation outline. It's how your website will look in Dreamweaver or Muse if you create an outline of the site. It basically shows how each page leads to the next. As you can see I put Blog as one page, where it's obviously a number of posts. The other permanent Pages on the site are separate.

- **Make a List of Pages to Create**

With your navigational structure outline, create a list of all the pages you need to create. This can include any pages that need to be added to the blog, any content that needs to be written for existing pages, and any Pages you may need in the future. Once they are outlined, add them to your content calendar.

- **What Don't Your Posts Cover?**

Before you start writing pages, ask yourself what you want your site to have that your posts do not cover. A page is permanent - it is a book on a shelf whereas your posts are articles in a newspaper. A post will fade into the background of your site over time (unless you link to it often, which we will cover shortly). A page is always up front and center. If there's something very important that you want to cover that you want people to see at all times, it should be on a page.

- **What Other Features/Services Do You Want to Include?**

Another reason you might create a page is because you offer a product or service you want to offer. For example, if you are a freelance writer or designer, you may have a separate page on your site so people can hire you. You also might have a page for your portfolio or another filled with contact information. These are all options depending on what the purpose of your blog is and what you do for a living.

Day 12 - Create a Comment List

Today's Goals:

Commenting is a great way to generate interest in your own site. Create comments on other sites and people will see those and link back to you or maybe just read whatever posts you wrote on that same topic.

Today I want to talk about not only where you will leave comments for other sites, but the comment policies you set up for your own site and how it will affect the flow of traffic to and from your site.

Why It's Important:

Commenting is one of those afterthoughts that a lot of bloggers forget about. A blog, like most online business ventures is about more than production. You can't produce and broadcast to people anymore. You have to interact with them at the same time and commenting is the way to do that through blogging.

Plus, you can't argue with the clear benefits of having people visit your site because they see all those comments you are posting on other peoples' sites. Not to mention the backlinks you can potentially get from blog writers by posting comments on their sites - how else will they know who you are if you don't respond to their posts?

To Do List:

• **Create a List of Sites to Comment On**

Using the blogs you've already checked out during your research as well as any others you looked at or have read recently, create a list of between 40 and 100 blogs that are similar to yours. These are sites where you can post comments on new topics that pop-up related to your website.

Once you have a list, start adding them to your RSS feed. You can use Google Reader or any of a number of other options such as FeedBurner to keep track of these sites. I like to have something installed on my desktop that tells me when a new post is available to read in my feed. This allows me to quickly pop in, read that post and leave a comment as I'm doing other work.

- **Generate a Commenting Schedule**

Depending on how you choose to comment, you may want to add this task to your schedule or content calendar. Personally, I do this throughout the week as I'm reading other blog posts. However, if you prefer to set aside an hour or two and work only on one thing at a time, you may want to create a schedule for when you will read other posts and comment on them. You can even create a reading list and go back and review those posts and leave comments at a later date.

- **Create Your Comment Policy**

You should also start thinking about what your comment policy will be. If you've not yet received your first comment, you don't necessarily need to worry about this yet. However, it's good to think about it early.

I allow pretty much any comments on my site (save spam, which Akismet catches). I will delete any phrases or words that are hateful or that attempt to incite violence, but other than that, I allow even the most negative of comments, so that I have a good opportunity to respond to them - it also tends to spur conversation from people who wouldn't otherwise comment.

- **Integrate Commenting CTAs into Your Content**

If you want people to leave more comments on your website, ask them to do it. Start adding calls to action to your content that ask people to comment on your content.

Try to be a little more creative than "please comment on my stuff" though. Ask for people to submit their own ideas based on a list you created. Ask people to submit anecdotes based on your own. Ask people to refute your opinions or to add to them if necessary. Think of creative ways to ask for comments and people will think of creative comments in turn.

Day 13 - Start Commenting

Today's Goals:

Okay so you have a nice big list of sites on which to comment. Now it is time to start commenting. Today's tasks will not be one time tasks. Like the writing, list building and review writing tasks we've already started these will become regular tasks that will help to build your site over time.

Specifically, we are going to start commenting on other blog posts and interacting with people actively on other sites, like Facebook and Twitter as well as other major blogs. The goal being to create an active conversation between you and other people in your niche that can one day send you traffic in turn.

Why It's Important:

Blogging is a social activity. Blogs are successful because they create ongoing relationships with people and drive traffic to and from multiple blogs. If you are really interested in having a large volume of traffic coming to your site, one of the first things you need to do is create a relationship with the people who visit your site. That's what today's tasks will do.

Like most of the stuff in this action plan, this needs to be done regularly to get the full effect. If you stop doing it because you are bored with it or because you don't feel you have time, you will lose an exponential source of traffic and credibility in your niche.

To Do List:

- **Post 3-5 Comments Per New Post You Write**

How many comments you post on other blogs will depend almost entirely on the number of posts you write for your own blog. However, if you don't read a lot of other blogs, I want you to set a minimum quota. For me, that quota is 3 to 5 comments for every new post that I write. This allows me to link directly to that post as well as the homepage and to grow the volume of traffic to my site.

- **Find 2-3 Thought Leader Blogs and Focus Your Efforts Here to Start**

At the same time, you shouldn't post your comments on dozens and dozens of blogs. If you have limited time, I recommend you choose two or three thought leaders in your niche and post a lot of comments on those blogs. At the same time, post a number of comments on various other blogs. You should have list of between 40 and 100 blogs to choose from, so make sure you're spreading your comment love equally among all of them.

- **Do the Same on Facebook and Twitter**

These days, one of the most effective ways to drive traffic back to your site is through social media. So don't limit your interaction to just blog comments. Look for ways to post comments to people's shares on Facebook and Twitter among other places. There are many options for how to interact with people on both Facebook and Twitter, but you need to make sure you're following those people as well.

- **Deep Link to Your Posts from These Comments**

Last but not least, make sure you are deep linking to your own posts from the comments you place. I don't recommend using anchor text names - use your real name - but you can use specific links to blog posts on your site. Look for ones that are specifically related to whatever post your comments. This is much easier if someone has the CommentLuv plugin, but you can still link to specific posts if they don't. Just make sure your comments offer real value to the readers of that blog.

I usually do three deep links and two homepage links for every five comments I leave on other blogs.

Day 14 - Social Media and RSS in the House

Today's Goals:

Let's not forget the other two big sources of traffic for most modern bloggers. RSS is a powerful way to keep people reading your blog content and social media is easily one of the most effective ways to drive traffic to your site over time. If you want people to reach out to you actively, you need to generate a clear way of doing so.

Today's goal is to generate an RSS feed and the tools needed for people to quickly signup for and follow that feed. Simultaneously, we want to create multiple social media outlets that you can use to generate links back to your content and to encourage people to further interact with your content.

Why It's Important:

Social media is just too powerful not to be used when generating traffic back to your blog. You want people to find you as quickly as possible and, more importantly, share that you exist with their friends or followers. Social media makes this immensely easy - allowing you to reach an exponentially growing audience rapidly with the right combination of targeted social marketing and a good volume of content.

To Do List:

- **Create Social Media Accounts for Your Blog**
If you haven't done it yet, create a social media account in Facebook, Twitter, LinkedIn, Google+ and YouTube for your blog. This should be different than the social media account you have set up for yourself. You will share all of

259

your posts here as well as information about your blog and any reviews you write.

- **Create an RSS Feed and Social Media Connections**

WordPress automatically generates an RSS feed, however, you need an external service to deliver that feed to readers. To do this, sign up for Feedburner and install a plugin on your website. There are number of other options available as well, but this is the easiest one to use and it allows you to monetize more effectively.

Once you've established your RSS feed, connect it to all of your social media accounts. This allows you to automatically post each blog post to those accounts. I like to customize the upload of any blog post to Facebook or Twitter, and you can do this by scheduling Facebook updates and tweets at the same time as you schedule your blog posts, but if you don't have time to do this automation is a very effective strategy. HootSuite is especially powerful for this.

- **Integrate CTAs into Your Blog for Both**

You can either create a permanent call to action at the bottom of every post by editing the single.php file or you can custom write one at the end of each post. The goal is to ensure that every blog post has a call to action at the end asking people to leave comments, and to sign up for your RSS feed or any social networks that you are on.

- **Create an Outline of Updates for Social Media**

You can add this to your content calendar if it's easiest for you, but create a short outline or calendar of when you'll update your social media accounts and what kind of content you will post. As you acclimate to using them for your business, you'll probably do this automatically. However, right now it's important that you remember to do it on a regular basis. Like with your blog, your social media accounts should be updated every single day.

260

You should also install apps for all of them on your phone so you can reply to comments or questions people leave you immediately.

Day 15 - The First Ads

Today's Goals:

It's not a mistake that we're now on day 15 and we have yet to post a single ad. I don't want you to think that advertising is the first focus of a good blog. Because content is what will allow you to monetize your blog at all, it needs to be the first focus. Only if you have quality content designed to generate hits and encourage participation will you successfully build a site big enough to actually make money.

Why It's Important:

This is an easy answer, but it's not as simple as you might think. Advertising is how you will monetize your blog and start making money, but today we are not going to blow up your blog into a massive ad platform. Today we are going to start advertising and thinking about what types of advertising and promotion work best with your content.

So, today's tasks are actually very important, ensuring that you don't jump the gun on ads and that the content you produce fits the needs of what you create.

To Do List:

• **Identify a Product You Can Promote**
The first marketing tactic I usually recommend is to write a review of a product related to the posts you've been writing. It's not overt advertising, it adds value to the blog, and you can have a conversation with your readers about it. These things are not true about display ads.

262

So, identify a product that relates closely to the topics you cover, while making sure it is something that you can personally recommend to people.

- **Write a Loose Review of that First Product**

Now write a review of that product. Again, I highly recommend you use the product before you write a review of it. This will make it easier to write a review and ensure that there's a level of trust between you and your readers.

When writing a review, follow the structure described here: http://bloggingwithjohnchow.com/membersarea/module-6-monetizing-01/affiliate-marketing/

It's a very simple structure, but it works well because it provides a balanced view of the product, while ending with a strong call to action. Keep in mind that you can write reviews for anything, not just affiliate products. For example, if you use a product you simply don't like, feel free to write a negative review to keep people from using it. This also adds value to your site.

- **Expand the Review and Include Images and Video (when applicable)**

Before posting your review, make sure it's one hell of a post. Add images where necessary, record a video if you feel comfortable doing so, and make sure the review is as extensive and comprehensive as possible. These are the most important posts on your site and need to be powerful and engaging. If you're lucky, it might even show up in Google for search terms related to the product name and author.

Day 16 - Content Upgrade

Today's Goals:

Let's not forget the goal of the content on your site - to be of as high of quality as possible. This stuff needs to positively hum with value, giving people as many reasons as possible to return to your website and keep reading. So, once you've gotten into the swing of things, it's time to find new ways to create engaging, interesting content.

When someone sees a video, they not only see high quality content, but they see me. They see the inside of my home and the life I live between writing blog posts for them to consume. It's a unique opportunity for my audience and a great way to provide added value, especially to people who may not like to read long posts.

That's what you need to do today - find a means by which to upgrade content quality on your site and provide something awesome.

Why It's Important:

Content is what you will build your site around, but it is only one piece of the puzzle. You could write two blog posts a day for 90 days and if they don't get seen by people or if they are derivative of another blog that has a bigger audience, you probably won't see that much growth.

At a certain point, whether you do it today or in three weeks, you need to think about how to upgrade content quality to a new level - one that people won't see on other sites. That is how you'll stand out and get the traffic you're looking for.

To Do List:

• **Make a List of Content Types You Can Create**

On one of the first days, I told you to make a list of the different types of content you can create. Now I want you to go one step further and make a list of the types of content you are not creating. Maybe you thought it would be fun to write different kinds of lists or make infographics. Now I want you to make a list of everything you have done, including videos, podcasting, long lists, comparison articles, reviews or responses to other blog posts.

You don't necessarily need to create all of this content, but you should eventually try everything at least once. Sometimes you'll find you actually enjoy something that you were previously uncomfortable doing. Other times, you will realize that a certain format is very much not for you. Both are okay, but it's good to explore all of your options.

• **List Previous Posts You Can Record or Rework**

Another cool thing about experimenting with the types of content you create is that you can convert old content into new content by changing formats. For example, you can take three or four blog posts and turn them into a podcast. Or, you can take one really long blog post and turn into an infographic. If you have any such posts, make a list today and think of ways you can record or rework them into new posts.

• **Ask Current Readers (or Friends and Family) for Ideas**

If you're drawing a blank on ways to upgrade your content or expand the site, simply ask your readers. If you don't have a lot of readers yet, ask your friends or family. Other people have very different ideas from you about what good content consists of. They might have ideas for how to make it more engaging or more entertaining, or there might be things that they've always wanted to see that they're hoping you will do.

- **Create One Unique Piece of Content for Your Calendar**

Now take a few minutes and put together a piece of content that matches the things we talked about about before. Tweak it, upgrade it, adjust it and make sure it's ready to change the format of your blog.

Day 17 - Connect with Other Bloggers

Today's Goals:

One of the coolest things about blogging is that it's not a solitary activity. You can work with other people in your niche, regardless of whether they are competitors or readers. This opens the floodgates for you to build relationships with dozens or even hundreds of other bloggers who are already talking about the things that are important to you and your audience.

Today the goal is to find as many of these blogs and bloggers as possible. Create a list of the people that you consider to be thought leaders in your niche, or that you respect and would like to know better. As a blogger, you will soon have the leverage needed to become a trusted member of their inner circle.

Why It's Important:

Like any business venture, the key to blogging success is in networking. The more people you know and the more effectively you get your name out there, the easier it will be to grow your audience and take advantage of opportunities that may not otherwise be there.

It is possible to grow a blog without networking with other bloggers. However, it takes longer, is significantly more time-consuming, and it's not quite as much fun. My first blog took off quickly because I was already a member of a booming forum community - had I not known anyone in my niche it would have taken much longer, especially if I wasn't willing to reach out to them.

267

If you're not comfortable talking to strangers, consider the many benefits of reaching out to people. I get a blast out of meeting new bloggers, either online or at conventions in person - I guarantee you will too.

To Do List:

- **Create a List of Bloggers in Your Niche**
A few days ago I had you create a list of blogs that are related to yours. Now I want you to go through and start creating a list of specific bloggers. While it's not necessarily easy to connect with specific people across multiple blogs, it is possible. So, create a list of the people that you would like to meet in person one day. It might be a few years from now, but if you have this list in hand, it will be easier to network with people online and to determine how you will network with them offline when the time comes.

- **Choose Three People You Want to Interview**
Another reason I like to create a list of actual people is that it allows me to see who I can interview or talk to directly. Choose three people from your list above that you would like to interview.

- **Choose Three People You Want to Be Interviewed By**
On the flip side, as your brand grows, you can also be interviewed by those people. It might not happen right away, but as your blog grows, your expertise will be in greater demand. People want to talk to you and want to learn more about what you do. Make a list of the people that you would love to be interviewed by.

- **Follow These Thought Leaders Actively**
It might take a while to make these things happen. However, the only way to ensure they do is to follow those people actively. Add all of their blogs to your

268

RSS feed, follow them on Facebook and Twitter, and post comments on any blog post they write. Keep in contact and I can guarantee that over time you will develop a strong relationship with them that translates to feature links, interviews and cool drinks at the next big industry convention.

Day 18 - Find Your Target Audience and Revise

Today's Goals:

In a lot of situations, we tend to project what we think about our audience before we actually look at who they are. The only way to know who they are, however how, is to get some traffic and see who shows up. So, now that you have built up a little traffic to your website, it's time to reach out to people who are visiting and find out what they are more interested in.

Why It's Important:

Obviously you want to write content for the people who visit your site. If you have preconceptions about who visits your site and it's different from the actual numbers, you're going to be creating content for people who aren't there. So, it's important that you constantly revise based on analytics and other data you gather for your site. You can even ask people what they want to see through comments or your email list.

To Do List:

- **Review Analytics**

There probably isn't enough data in Analytics yet to make any clear decisions. We'll take a closer look at this later in the month. However, you can take your first look at Analytics today, ensuring that is installed on your blog, and that data is being gathered.

NOTE: If you have not done so yet, sign up for Analytics and install it on your blog with the Ultimate Google Analytics WordPress plugin. It should take less than five minutes and it will start gathering data within a half an hour.

270

- **Note Popular Keywords**

As soon as you start gathering data, take a look at the keywords that people search for to find your website. It might be that your website is not yet indexed in Google or that you are not receiving a lot of search traffic. However, return here often to see what types of keywords people use to find your site. This can help you determine what to write about in the future.

- **Compare to Your Content Calendar**

Take a look at your content calendar and see if the topics listed match the keywords people are searching for to find your website. The goal is to write content that matches who is actually looking for it. You may start seeing patterns that will cause you to adjust what you write.

- **Check Comment and Share Numbers on Posts**

Again, you might not see a lot of comments or share numbers on your posts just yet. However, keep a close eye on these numbers. Start checking every day to see what comments and shares you've received. If a blog post gets a lot of feedback, it's probably because it's a topic people care about. If this is the case, it should be something you return to frequently. At the same time, don't overdo something because it seems popular, especially if its not an evergreen topic. News topics in particular can be hot for a few hours and then die.

- **Send Out a Survey on the Blog and in Email**

As your blog grows and your email list expands, don't be afraid to send a survey to subscribers and ask them what they think. As soon as you have 20 subscribers on your email list, ask them what types of topics they like to see you on the blog. You can also do the same in a blog post asking people to leave comments requesting specific topics.

271

Day 19 - What's Working?

Today's Goals:

Some things work when you create a new website and some things don't. Yesterday you looked at Analytics and thought about what types of things are working for your site in terms of the audience and topics you cover. Today I want to dig deeper into those numbers and into the way the site is built.

The goal today is to review everything you have done thus far and ensure that it is working for you. This is not a chance to overhaul your entire blog - that's a bad idea and can lead to a cycle of constant revision that never really ends. But you can look at how the site is being built, whether you are meeting your deadlines and whether the traffic is starting to justify the time spent.

Why It's Important:

As a website owner it's important that you regularly review what works and what doesn't. As I said, you can't just change everything on a weekly basis, however, you can review the assumptions you previously made and determine whether they were correct or need revision.

I've made a boatload of decisions about my websites that turned out to be bad. I'm willing to admit that, however, and make changes to ensure I don't repeat those mistakes and to fix whatever damages were done by the original mistake. This is where you do the same.

To Do List:

- **Is Your Content Calendar Working**
Based on the data you've been gathering, do you feel that your content

calendar is working? More specifically, are you able to keep up with the content calendar you wrote a week ago? If not, today is the day to make some revisions. Break it down and make sure that you're not asking yourself to do more than you reasonably can. Be realistic and set tough goals but don't set such tough goals that you consistently fall behind.

- **What Are People Saying**

Take into consideration what people are telling you as well. If people feel your blog posts are rushed, poorly researched, or are not showing up frequently enough, this is feedback you should take into account.

- **Setting Long Term and Short Term Goals**

A goal is a dream with actionable tasks that can make it a reality. So, make sure that your goals directly reflect your dreams. Do you want to make a lot of money and quit your day job? Or are you interested more in providing valuable information to people in your niche? At the same time, there may be other short-term goals that you need to accomplish first, such as making enough money to justify the time spent on the blog.

- **Ensuring You're Being Fair to Your Expectations**

Set realistic expectations and ensure that you're being fair to yourself. Don't expect yourself to write ten blog posts a week when you only have an hour to spend each day. At the same time, push yourself. Ideally, you should come up just short or just ahead of your goals every week. You should never overshoot them too far nor should you underperform to such a level that the content quality suffers.

Day 20 - Linking to Other Sites

Today's Goals:

It was believed for a long time that linking to other websites could somehow hurt your own. However, linking to other websites is seen by Google as a value adding tactic. The key is to ensure that any website you link to is actually directly related to what you're talking about. At the same time, you should avoid linking directly to competitors who offer the exact same content as you. Today I want to talk about the best way to link to other sites and how it can improve your rankings in Google and won't harm the readership on your site.

Why It's Important:

The Internet is littered with opinions and ideas about how best to build a website, where links should go and where they shouldn't. However, at the end of the day, the most important thing about your site is that it's usable and user-friendly. So, I want you to ignore anything you've heard before and instead focus on what you think will make your website more effective and user-friendly for your visitors. In this case, that may include adding links to other websites that offer more in-depth information or detailed analysis of a topic you're covering.

To Do List:

•   **Record Sources for Each Post You Write**
No doubt, as you surf the Internet looking for information about a specific topic for a post, you write down a lot of different things from other websites. It might be how something is worded, an opinion of a thought leader, or

274

something else that you just didn't know, but this offers an opportunity for you to include a number of links to other sources.

Whenever you write a new post, keep a list of all the websites you reference or research for that post. You don't necessarily need to create a list or bibliography for every post you write, but you can link to some of those pages within your post to provide value to your readers.

- **Identify Where to Add Links**

Go back through your old posts and look for places where you can add new links. It might be a section that you skimmed through really quick to find something or it could be an area where you reference news article or a speech given by a thought leader in your niche. In any of these cases you can link to the original source and provide instant value your readers.

- **Avoid Non-Useful Links or Cash-Only Links**

The key to linking to other content on your site is to ensure that it is actually valuable. Not only are you risking people leaving your site for good if you don't provide something useful, but you're driving them to another site.

You should also avoid links that are designed to make you money. While it is okay to post an affiliate link in a review or in a situation in which somebody knows that it's an affiliate link, I don't recommend hiding them inside a blog post. There are exceptions to this rule, especially as your site grows and ages, but as you're getting started, avoid it.

- **Target Bloggers that Can Reciprocate**

One of the most effective ways to use links on your site is to target other blogs. When you post a link to another blog, that blogger will receive a Pingback. This tells them you linked to their content. They can then read your content and in many cases they might reciprocate. This is a very effective way to grow the number of links to your site.

Day 21 - Deep Linking and Natural Linking

Today's Goals:

We're going to switch gears today. Keep writing and commenting and sharing, but instead of another structural change, today I want to talk about your first encounter with SEO.

Search engine optimization for a blog is relatively simple. You will be spending hours and hours building back links or tweaking the content on your site. Wordpress is incredibly search engine friendly and back links come in relatively fast, especially when you're leaving lots of comments and encouraging people to share your content.

But there are quite a few things you can do, so I want to talk about the first of those today. Deep and natural linking are what will eventually drive the most traffic to your site.

Why It's Important:

Google has said time and again that the most effective way to rise in the search rankings is to have high-quality content that provides value to your readers. However, you also need do a few other things, especially if you're in a highly competitive niche with a lot of other bloggers and site owners who are doing the same. That's why I am a big fan of deep linking within my posts, as well as natural linking from outside sources. These provide context for Google when ranking your content and ensure you appear for as many keywords as possible within your niche.

To Do List:

- **Review Existing Posts for Link Opportunities**

Look through all of your existing posts for opportunities to add deep links. Deep linking is only effective once you have a large enough volume of posts on your site. You can't link to other posts when you only have one or two. However, now that you have nearly 15 to 20 posts, you should start linking between them.

- **Add 5-10 Deep Links Per Post**

Starting with your newest posts, and periodically going back and adding old posts, add between five and ten links to every post.

For a long time there were concerns that too many links on a single page could hurt. And while it is possible to over link a page, it's hard to do. Five to ten links on a single 500 word post is a perfectly safe number.

- **Ensure Share Buttons Are Active on Every Post**

WordPress does not yet come with Facebook, Twitter and LinkedIn buttons built-in. So, you need to download a plug-in and add it to your blog. Make sure you do this as soon as possible as it allows people to immediately share the content on your site with others. This is free publicity - don't ignore its value.

- **Build a List of Sites on Which You Want Links**

You have long had a list of blogs and now bloggers that you want to interact with. You can promote your content specifically to those blogs. So, create a list of blogs on which you want links. These should be sites with high Page Ranks in your niche that discuss topics either directly or indirectly related to yours.

- ### **Start Promoting Yourself and Your Content to Those Sites**

Now, when you write new content, either link it to those blogs listed above, or find ways to interact with those bloggers by posting comments on their sites or interacting with them on Facebook or Twitter.

Day 22 - Advertising?

Today's Goals:

I've mentioned this quite a few times, but I'll repeat it here. When you first build a blog, you shouldn't have ads on it. Advertising assumes a certain level of trust between you and your readers that doesn't develop overnight. You need to cultivate it over time and build the quality of the content on your site, something you have not yet done, even after three weeks.

But, seeing as how we are closing out three weeks and you have content for most of that time (hopefully close to 15-20 posts now), you are probably starting to get some steady traffic and I want to talk about how you will start to advertise when you are ready.

Why It's Important:

This is where the money comes in. If you want to turn your blogging hobby into a blogging business, you need a means to monetize and for most of you, that will be through ads.

279

This is my blog's homepage and there are quite a few ads. I have a banner across the top, banners on the right side bar, a built-in ad with each post and I write affiliate reviews of products all the time.

So, how do you do the same without alienating your audience? Here is a quick synthesis of what we talked about in the book and how you'll start doing this when it is time to monetize.

To Do List:

• **Create a List of What You Will Promote**
Start making a list of products you want to promote. For now, it can just be a list of books you like, info products you use, or products on Amazon that you'd like to promote to your readers. Ideally, all of these products should be things that you like and have used so that you can write a realistic and trustworthy review about them.

• **Define Where Ads Can Be Placed**
Start asking yourself where you want ads to be placed on your website. Do you want just a handful of them on the sidebar or are you willing to sell larger volumes of space on the front page to finance your efforts?

• **Create Editorial Guidelines for Reviews**
Reviews should follow your own strict editorial guidelines. Specifically, what are you willing to promote and how are you willing to describe it? For the most part, the answers will depend on how you want your readers to read these. If you want people to take you seriously, you should write reviews that are realistic and based on personal experience. They should include pros and cons and should be built around the premise that you want to help people make a good buying decision, not just make sales on your site.

- **Add the Necessary Disclaimers to Your Site**

Today is a good day to add disclaimers to your website. Many countries require that you have disclaimers whenever you sell something or make claims about profit. You should have a privacy policy along with an earnings disclaimer and terms of service. The earnings disclaimer is very important, and should be prominent. Whenever you promote a product, make sure people understand that you could make money if they click on that link and that any results shown are yours alone and are not always typical of the product.

- **Write Your First Review for Your Content Calendar**

Start writing your first review. A good review should be based on personal experience, and should show people exactly why you are recommending the product. A blind recommendation is not as powerful as you might think. Especially when you're just starting your blog, people don't know who you are, you need to build trust, both with the recommendation and with the way you review it.

Day 23 - Get More Immediate Traffic

Today's Goals:

There are two types of traffic online. There is the slow and steady traffic that you will build up by ranking in organic search results. Then there is the quick and (kind of but not really) easy traffic. This is the stuff you get from people sharing your content with their friends, advertising on Google or Facebook, or a post that happens to get shared or reposted on a major blogging site.

A lot of this stuff you don't control. However, there are some things you can do to increase the volume of immediate traffic you get and the frequency of these immediate traffic boosts. Today I want to talk about some of those things and how you can do them right now, even with a brand new blog.

Why It's Important:

The slow and steady approach is very effective. However, it can be incredibly frustrating, especially when you consider that most blogs take between six and twelve months to reach the kind of traffic volume needed before you can even think about monetizing. If you can fast-track that, increasing your traffic dramatically through viral posts, sharing or even through paid traffic you can build your business much faster.

To Do List:

• **What's Your Budget?**

Do you have a budget? If you have no budget, as most bloggers don't when starting, paid advertising is probably out of the question. There are other options to get immediate traffic, but keep in mind that paid advertising can be

282

costly, and generally speaking does not pay itself back unless you have a monetization plan in place already.

- **Identify Your Prime Sharing Opportunities**

So, if your budget is zero, or if you'd like to minimize how much money you spend, start by identifying the prime sharing opportunities in your niche. Specifically, what are people who read your blog most likely to share? Do they like pictures of cats with funny captions, or do they prefer complicated lists of technical topics? Find the trigger point by following some of these people on Twitter and Facebook and seeing what they most often share - now you can start emulating that content.

- **How Can You Distribute Content**

Make a list of different ways you can distribute content to people in your niche. There are number of ways to do that. Facebook, Twitter, LinkedIn, Google+, YouTube and other social networks are the usually the first places to look. However, there are other options, including:

* Scribd
* Squidoo
* Tumblr
* Hubspot
* Blogger

- **Create a Viral Approach Plan**

There's no way to guarantee anything you create will go viral. However, as you better understand your audience, you can create content that is more likely to be shared rapidly and subsequently go viral.

Start by creating a list of possible content types that you know people like. Examples include long list of items (e.g "101 ways to..."), funny graphics, infographics, videos, or diatribes on possibly controversial topics.

Now decide which of these possible content types will work best for your content and think of topics that will fit them.

• **Start Experimenting**

Viral content often develops with a little bit of luck and a lot of research. So, start experimenting with different content types. Truly viral content often takes a lot of time to create. However, you can test the waters by creating smaller, simpler versions of larger projects and seeing how people respond to them. If you create an info graphic and it gets two or three times as many shares as a normal post, you know that this is a good place to start.

See how your audience responds to any one type of content, and then use that response to inform how you create new content in the future.

Day 24 - Brainstorm Guest Post Opportunities

Today's Goals:

This goes really well with yesterday's task. Just posting is one of the most effective ways to build your brand, increase the trust people have in you as a blogger, and get immediate traffic. However, getting a guest post opportunity is not easy. You have to reach out to other bloggers, prove to them that you have valuable content they might be interested in, and then actually get them to agree to post your content.

Today, I want you to brainstorm some guest post opportunities, as well as some content you can write for those posts. This may not happen overnight, it might take a few weeks before you get your first guest post, but when you do it will improve the visibility of your site dramatically.

Why It's Important:

Guest posting is a very effective way to boost traffic to your site, improve the quality of back links pointing to your site and ensure that the people visiting your site already knew who you are and trust the opinions you offer.

Plus it's great for SEO, improving the organic search rankings of your site.

To Do List:

• **Create a List of Sites You Want to be On**
Not every site is a good fit for the content you write. So, create a list of sites on which you want to see posts written by yourself. Of course, not every site accepts guest posts. So, you should check their guest posting editorial

guidelines, or email the site owner directly and ask before going to the trouble of writing and submitting a post.

You can check pretty easily by doing a Google blog search and using the term "guest post" to see which posts are written by a guest.

- **Research Those Sites for Topics Related to Yours**

Now, what you have a list of sites on which you want to be featured, go through those sites and look for content that is similar to your own. The goal is to write content that appeals to the audience of both that site and your own. If you write a blog about dog training, you probably wouldn't go to a site about how to build a computer and write a blog post about choosing a new motherboard.

However, you could go to blog about training agility dogs, and write a post about how to start training an agility dog from a puppy.

- **Make a List of Topics You Can Write About**

With that information in hand make a list of topics you can write about. Brainstorm, spend some time developing content, and create a long list of content that you can forward to other people.

- **Write 1-3 Posts for Guest Opportunities**

Most guest posting opportunities require you to write the content in advance. Because you have to write the content in advance, you will spend time researching that blog and understanding what they need. Most blogs will not tell you what they need ahead of time.

So, sit down and write 1-3 blog posts based on the guest posting opportunities you've created. If you're not sure what to write about, you can always email those blog owners and ask them for topic ideas. However, don't be surprised if they don't reply.

- **Create a Query Letter for those Posts and Send Them**

Once you've written a post for another blog, it's time to write a query letter for that blog owner. Keep in mind that you should not submit one guest post to multiple blogs. The last thing you want to do it accidentally have it posted to multiple sites and have them think that you're sending out duplicate content.

Personalize these letters as much as possible. You want to reach people directly, creating a link between you and them and not sending out a blank form letter that looks too sterile.

Day 25 - Monetizing Part 2

Today's Goals:

The other day we talked about your first ads. For most of you, the first add on your site will be an affiliate review or something similar. Posting large ads on your site that don't have integrated calls to action will just drive traffic away from your content. However, at a certain point, you'll want to put real ads on your site. For most of you, that won't come for a few more weeks.

Why It's Important:

Advertising is huge. This is how you're going to make most of your money. So, even though you're probably a few days or even weeks away from being ready for display ads on your site, it's a good idea to have a plan in place for where those ads will go, how many you will place, and which networks and products you are comfortable promoting.

Heck, if you have the traffic, you can even place some ads right now. However, keep in mind that prioritizing ads over content is a sure way to drive down traffic and keep your site in that limbo state where you don't quite make enough money to justify all that time being spent.

To Do List:

• **Identify Where to Place Ads**

Where do you want the ads to be placed on your site? A website has a lot of real estate to work with, but you don't necessarily want to use it all for your ads. So, decide where you want them.

Here's what my site looks like:

288

I've placed ads at the very top, along the right side bar and embedded in each post. People don't mind ads (most people anyways) and are generally used to them, so don't be afraid to put them where they make sense.

•   Decide What You Will Promote

Make a list of what you want to promote. You already have a list of products you want to promote on your site. Now, spend some time generating a list of other things you can promote. Services you like (I recommend HostGator to people, for example), products you like from Amazon, or info products you've had success with.

•   Set Value Targets for Each Ad Spot

If you plan on placing ads on your site in permanent spots, determine what those spots will be and what their value is. The value of an ad spot when sold directly is usually determined by the number of impressions that page of your site generates.

Check BuySellAds.com to learn more about how these page views are priced and what people are willing to pay for impressions in your niche.

- **Amazon, Clickbank, AdSense?**

Finally, decide what forms of monetization you would like to use for your site. There are quite a few options to choose from, so choose ones that match the types of products you like and the format you prefer to promote.

Day 26 - Comment Boosting Hat Trick

Today's Goals:

You been doing this for a few weeks now, and you might be getting a little frustrated that nobody's commenting on your posts. Keep in mind that on average between 0.1% and 1% of visitors will post a comment after reading a post. Our goal is to keep that number as close to 1% as possible, rather than the one among thousands that the most people get.

Today we will do a few things to improve the number of comments you get and to ensure the comments you do get are of the highest possible quality.

Why It's Important:

Why do we care about comments? Because, comments represent the engagement of your audience with your site, and they look really good to your newest visitors. They also give you an opportunity show off your knowledge, to handle any negative feedback you might receive, and to show people that you are engaged with the readers.

To Do List:

• **Review Past Posts for High Comment Counts**
This may not apply right away, but once you have a few posts and those posts are starting to generate comments, review the posts that get a lot of comments for common factors. What specifically is causing that post to get more comments than any other?

• **Integrate a CTA into Each Post**
Go back and add a called action to all of your posts. Future posts should also

291

contain a call to action. It should be specific to that post. For example, ask people to submit ideas similar to your own in a post or ask them to submit arguments that refute yours.

- **Open Up Your Commenting Policy**

Many blogs start with a very restrictive commenting policy. Moderation, censorship and other factors can greatly reduce the number of comments you receive. On my site, the only policy I have in place is that I won't except vulgarity or hateful words in the comments. In many cases I still allow the comments to exist, and just edit them slightly. Make sure your comment policy is as open and accepting as possible and your comment numbers will increase dramatically.

- **Increase Comments on Other Sites**

Decide how many comments you want to post on other sites. Today you should post a handful of comments on the blogs you read most often. Any posts you read should get a comment. Even if you don't have a strong opinion about a topic get in the habit of commenting on it anyway. Ask yourself what you can add to the conversation, or what questions you have for the writer. Getting into a habit of conversing with other bloggers will make it easier to converse with your own readers when they start commenting on your posts.

- **Hold a Comment Contest**

You don't have to do this now, and in fact you should probably wait until your comment count is a little higher and your readership increases, but a contest can greatly increase the number of comments you receive. The rule should state that anybody who leaves a comment is automatically entered in the contest. You can define how you will choose a winner any way you want, but make sure that comments are all accepted equally to encourage people to chime in.

- **Write a Post Based on Comments**

Again, this can wait until you have a few more comments on your site, but it is a very effective way to build content and encourage more comments. Iv'e seen this work quite well on quite a few blogs with higher readership numbers. Create a weekly Q&A session based on comments that include questions. You can also write an entire post based on an idea that someone submits in a comment. Just make sure to give credit where due.

Day 27 - Review Analytics and Revise Your Plans

Today's Goals:

One of the most powerful tools you have at your disposal is Google Analytics. Google Analytics provides countless volumes of data that you can use to tweak and improve the efficiency and effectiveness of your website. So, you should be looking at it every single day. Today I want to take a closer look at some of the statistics in Google Analytics and how you can use them to change your plans and improve your site based on real data instead of intuition.

Why It's Important:

Over time, you're going to make a lot of judgment calls. Some of these will involve what type of content to write, while others will be about monetization or commenting strategies. However, there are certain things you can decide based on real raw data. That's where Google Analytics comes in. Using the data, you can make informed, educated decisions instead of random guesses.

To Do List:

- ### Choose a Time Frame for Review
Don't review data randomly. Pick specific periods of time and look at them in comparison to other periods of time. For example, you are now getting to the end of the first month. So, in the future you can compare this first month of data to other months of data. You can also review on a weekly basis. Remember, however, that if you narrow your focus too much, often the data is not significant enough to provide valuable information.

- **Look for Patterns in the Data**

Look for simple patterns in the data. Spending too much time analyzing large volumes of data can create headaches and generally doesn't give you any insight. However, some patterns will be more obvious than others.

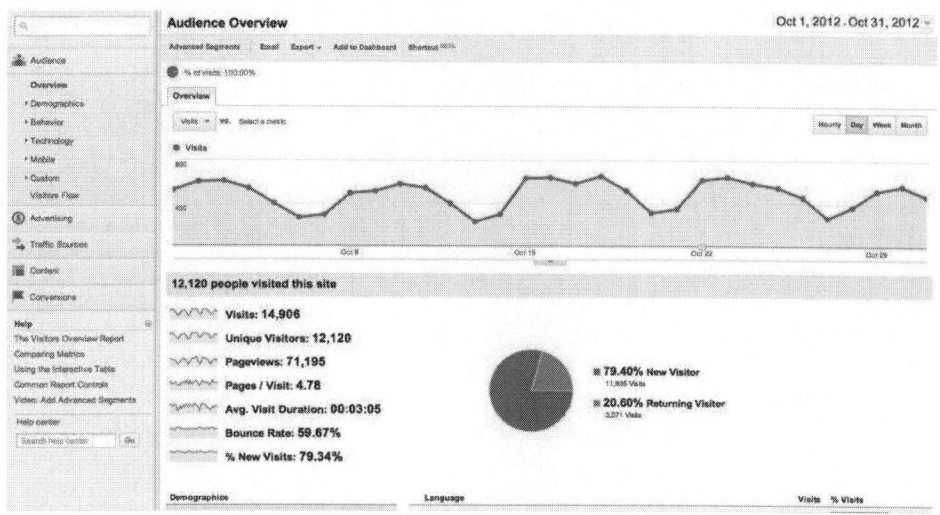

Take this for example. As we can see, traffic increases dramatically during the middle of the week. It decreases dramatically on the weekend. So, if I have a post that is very important, I'm going to post it on a Wednesday or Thursday when traffic is at its highest. Look for similar patterns in your data.

- **Make a List of Changes You Can Make**

Based on what you see, make a list of changes you can make. If you don't see anything you can change, no problem. In fact, not changing things is as much a sign of success as anything else. However, if anything is underperforming your goals, or if you feel you can further improve a number, look for ways to do so.

Split testing is incredibly effective in this way, and can be done to a variety of things on your site, including the layouts, navigation structure, placement of ads, headline size and placement, and excerpt length.

Day 28 - Adsense On Your Site?

Today's Goals:

A lot of people ask me whether Google AdSense is a good thing to add to their website. Generally speaking, I'm not a fan of AdSense on a new website. Of course, I don't like ads on any new website. For this reason, a lot of people assume that AdSense isn't good. However, in certain circumstances, AdSense can be a great way to improve the value of the content you post. Today I want to talk about when AdSense makes sense and when you can start making real money from it.

Why It's Important:

Google AdSense is by far one of the easiest advertising tools to integrate into your website. On a very basic level it can be done in as little as five minutes. However, that's the major problem. Most people add Google AdSense their site, forget about it, and never upgrade or tweak it to ensure it is providing the most valuable ads possible. My goal is to ensure that doesn't happen to you.

To Do List:

• **Is AdSense Right for You?**
Google AdSense is not a good fit for every website. So, ask yourself today whether you are interested in having it on your site or not. If you'd prefer to have higher-quality ads for specific products you want to promote, you should avoid placing Google AdSense on your site for now. At the same time, Google AdSense is really only profitable when the traffic is there to support it. So, if traffic is still an issue, you may want to put this on ice for a few days or weeks.

297

- **Create Your Campaign**

All you need to create an AdSense campaign is a Google account. So, use your Google account to login to Google AdSense and start building your first campaign. Keep in mind that for any one website you can only have three blocks of ads. So, create three separate ad blocks and assign them their own custom channel. This will ensure you can track them and see what the bidding gap is. In many cases, it might make sense only to have a single block on your site.

- **Decide What Sections of Content Will Reflect the Ads**

Google makes it easy to define what parts of the content on your site will be inspected to match the ads. So, decide right now what sections of existing posts you'd like to have represented by the ads. You should then start integrating these tags into your posts whenever you write them. Read more about this here.

- **Set Competitive Filters**

Start adding competitive websites or Made for AdSense sites to your filters. This will ensure that sites designed to steal traffic from your site or show low-quality ads that link to low-quality sites are removed immediately before they have a chance to appear. This offers greater value to your readers and ensures you don't lose traffic to sites that offer no value.

Day 29 - Content Calendar Revision

Today's Goals:

Now that we're almost at the end of the first month, it's time to take a look back at your content calendar. Because you built your content calendar in the first week, you might find that you have different ideas about what you want to post and what your audience wants to read. Today is the day when you sit down and make revisions based on your recent experiences.

Generally speaking, I do this every 3 to 6 months. I've been blogging for a very long time, however, so I have a much better idea of what people in my niche are looking for. Because you're just getting started, I recommend that you take a look at your content calendar every 2-4 weeks. This will ensure that you can make changes as they are needed.

Why It's Important:

A good content calendar captures what people are interested in right now. That's why I never go out more than one month. Having 3-4 months worth of outlines means that you could be writing about something people are no longer interested in three months from now. At the same time, going a month out ensures that you have content ready to go even if a major problem develops that keeps you from posting.

To Do List:

• **Review the Posts You Wrote**

Take a quick look through all the content you've written this month. Ignore your current content calendar and look only at the things you've published. You want to get a good idea for the flow of content. Did you cover a topic multiple times? Are there any topics that you feel you covered too much? What about not enough? Make notes about things you'd like to change or things that did or did not work during the last month.

- **Remove Anything That Didn't Work**

If there are topics or formats that you did not like or that your readers did not like, consider removing them from your content calendar, at least temporarily. In the future, you can put them back in if you want to test something new, but for now the goal is to find the things that will work most effectively.

- **Increase Anything That Did Work**

If a post was extremely successful, such as a video or comprehensive list, consider how you can integrate it into your site more frequently. Add more of these types of posts to your content calendar, or choose a day of the week to focus on that type of content - a video blog Tuesday or infographic Friday.

- **Look for Opportunities to Improve**

As a website owner, you should be looking for ways to improve content quality on a regular basis. Whether it is developing a new type of content or removing something from your calendar that readers clearly are not interested in reading, there are always opportunities to improve what you publish and how it is read by your readers.

Day 30 - Taking it to the Next Level

Today's Goals:

Congratulations! You just made it one month into your first blog. In that time, you've developed more than a dozen pages of content, developed a working relationship with your first readers, and started to meet and work with other bloggers in your niche. You've done more in 30 days than many bloggers do in their first year. And for this reason, I know for fact that you're going to be successful.

But you're not done yet. The first 30 days is arguably the hardest, but it doesn't get that much easier. While you're going to start learning what people want, how to respond to comments and how to build your audience much faster, you're also going to learn that running a blog is a lot of work. You have to maintain strict deadlines, ensure that you're constantly online so you can respond to comments, and building relationships with people in your niche.

Today I want to talk about some of the things you should keep in mind as you move into the future. These are tasks and big goals that you're going to have in mind as you grow the traffic to your site and start monetizing.

Why It's Important:

You can never be too prepared for an opportunity when it comes to blogging. There will always come a time when you need to take your blogging to the next level and if you have already clearly outlined what you will do when that time comes, your life will be that much easier (and your blog that much more successful).

To Do List:

- **When to Monetize**

When you monetize will depend on traffic and readership. To most bloggers I recommend monetization by the end of the first month. However, I also recommend against any types of monetization that involve clicking away from a website. As your readership grows, the last thing you want is for people to leave your site when they should be getting to know you a little better.

For this reason, the answer is different for every person reading this action plan. If you're interested in monetizing immediately, focus on ads that don't drive traffic away and will build trust. These include reviews and recommendations for products your personal use.

- **Content Volume Increases**

As content volume increases and your readership grows, opportunities to advertise and monetize will grow with them. At the same time, don't rely solely on the volume of content to help you determine when to monetize.

- **When Will It Make Me Money?**

I get this question all the time, and it really depends on your site, your readership, how effectively you monetize, and how often you review and revise the plans you make for your site. I managed to turn my current website into a profitable one within a month. At the same time, other blogs take much longer. There is no minimum or maximum amount of time to start making money with a blog, but if you follow the tips in this action plan and the main book, I can guarantee that with time you will start to make a profit.

- **Hours Per Week Invested**

At the same time, the number of hours per week will directly affect how much money you make. For example, the number of page views your website gets will depend on how many posts you have and how many readers read each of those posts. If you only post once per week, the volume of page views is directly tied to the number of visitors. The more often you post, the more page views you get and the more you can charge for advertising.

If you haven't yet, sit down and think about how much time you want to invest in your website. Don't think of it in terms of total return on investment, but as the amount of energy and time you can safely put in while still enjoying the blogging process.

How to Win the Blogging Game

I've been at this a long time - more than 10 years - and Peng Joon has been at it almost equally as long. In that time, we have created a business model that just plain works.

The idea is simple. Create a hub focused on delivering value to your readers. Build, build, build and then monetize. It's no coincidence that Google has decided the exact same thing and SEO's everywhere are scrambling to catch up.

We never had to catch up. Quality has always been part of the formula and now you have that exact same formula in front of you - one that will work over and over again in any niche with any audience.

The key is your persistence and passion. If you can create a quality product that you feel strongly about and ensure that it remains at the top of the search listings, the money will come naturally.

No need to chase people and find the "next big thing" - just be the best at what you do and write or record content that reflects it.

Blogging is not a fad. It only continues to grow stronger and gain legitimacy in the eyes of news media and journalists everywhere. Internet marketers have for some reason ignored it though - probably because it takes so much time.

We're here to tell you that blogging, time investment or no is one of the most effective ways to make money online.

Content sells - to the search engines, to your prospects and to the product vendors you're eager to promote.

Enjoy your journey... we've certainly enjoyed paving the path.

Here's to your future success in the blogosphere!

John Chow and Peng Joon

Printed in Great Britain
by Amazon.co.uk, Ltd.,
Marston Gate.